SCIENCE
DETECTIVES

OXFORD
UNIVERSITY PRESS

Great Clarendon Street, Oxford OX2 6DP

Oxford University Press is a department of the University of Oxford.
It furthers the University's objective of excellence in research, scholarship,
and education by publishing worldwide in

Oxford   New York

Auckland   Cape Town   Dar es Salaam   Hong Kong   Karachi
Kuala Lumpur   Madrid   Melbourne   Mexico City   Nairobi
New Delhi   Shanghai   Taipei   Toronto

With offices in

Argentina   Austria   Brazil   Chile   Czech Republic   France   Greece
Guatemala   Hungary   Italy   Japan   Poland   Portugal   Singapore
South Korea   Switzerland   Thailand   Turkey   Ukraine   Vietnam

Oxford is a registered trade mark of Oxford University Press
in the UK and in certain other countries

British Library Cataloguing in Publication Data

Data available

ISBN: 978-0-19-911974-5

Originated and created for Oxford University Press
by the Brown Reference Group

1 3 5 7 9 10 8 6 4 2

Printed in China

SCIENCE DETECTIVES

Mike Goldsmith

Blazing a Trail

OXFORD
UNIVERSITY PRESS

TABLE OF CONTENTS

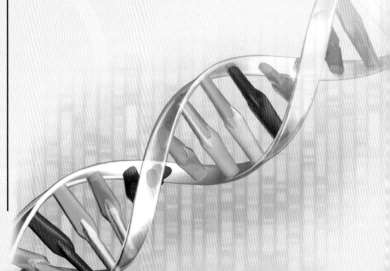

WHAT IS SCIENCE?

FOR CENTURIES, SCIENTISTS HAVE STUDIED THE WORLD JUST LIKE DETECTIVES, COLLECTING EVIDENCE FOR THEIR THEORIES. IN DOING THIS, AND BY MAKING THAT KNOWLEDGE AVAILABLE TO EVERYONE, THEY HAVE ALSO CHANGED THE WORLD.

Science is an amazingly powerful tool that we use to help us understand the Universe. The word also refers to the knowledge we gain by using that tool – 'science' comes from the Latin word for knowledge, *scientia*.

Scientific explanations are special because they can be proved or disproved. They are only generally accepted after they have been carefully tested. This ability to explain the things that happen in the world around us gives science enormous power.

▲ *Scientists develop theories that explain as many things as possible. The same theory that explains lightning and how it works also helped scientists to make light bulbs.*

▲ *Some scientific discoveries were made hundreds of years ago. For example, the Chinese found out how to make fireworks in the 12th century.*

Newton said he had seen further than others by 'standing on the shoulders of giants'.

Even the greatest scientists can only build on the work of their predecessors.

CHANGING LIVES

A world without science is hard to imagine. Not only would we have no mobile phones, MP3 players, computers or transport, we would have no proper clothes either. Without medical science to keep us healthy and technology to provide food for us, most of us would not even be alive. But science does not just help us to survive, it is also the key to an understanding of ourselves and the world in which we live. Scientific discoveries have told us how and why the Earth developed over billions of years, and have sent people and machines out into space to explore the Universe and find out about its origins.

THE WORLD OF SCIENCE

THE HUGE WORLD OF SCIENCE COVERS MANY DIFFERENT SUBJECTS. HOWEVER, IT CAN BE DIVIDED INTO THE BRANCHES OF PHYSICS, CHEMISTRY, BIOLOGY AND MATHEMATICS.

The world of science has led to a world of technology, so physics gives us vehicles; chemistry, clothes; biology, food; and maths, computers. The world of science is also a world of people. Some, like most of the people in this book, spend their lives working as scientists. But looking at the stars, drawing plants or collecting stones can also be science. So anyone can be a scientist, because science is not what you do, it is how you do it.

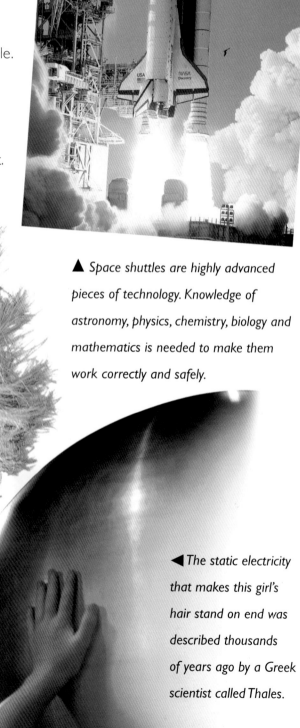

▲ Space shuttles are highly advanced pieces of technology. Knowledge of astronomy, physics, chemistry, biology and mathematics is needed to make them work correctly and safely.

◄ The static electricity that makes this girl's hair stand on end was described thousands of years ago by a Greek scientist called Thales.

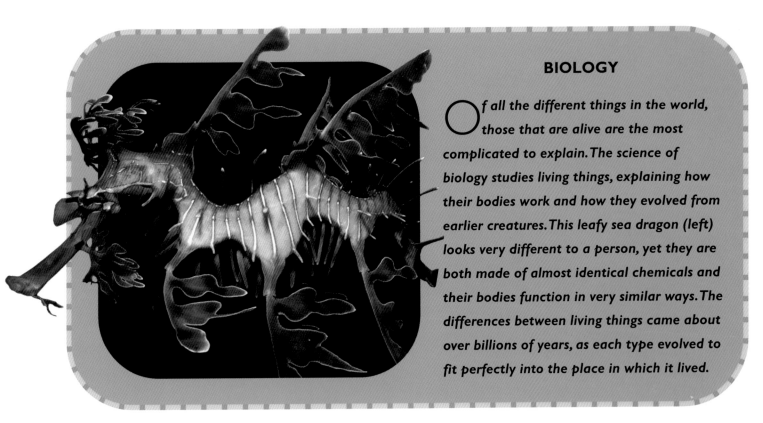

BIOLOGY

Of all the different things in the world, those that are alive are the most complicated to explain. The science of biology studies living things, explaining how their bodies work and how they evolved from earlier creatures. This leafy sea dragon (left) looks very different to a person, yet they are both made of almost identical chemicals and their bodies function in very similar ways. The differences between living things came about over billions of years, as each type evolved to fit perfectly into the place in which it lived.

► Chemistry is not just about drugs and test tubes. Chemical tests of gases collected from volcanoes tell us about the mysterious interior of the Earth.

LOOK CLOSER

Mathematics is important in all areas of science. One of the mysteries of science is that the world seems to behave in the simplest possible way that mathematics can describe.

The Erekthion on the Acropolis was built as a temple to mark the
spot where the Greek goddess Athena triumphed over the god
Poseidon in a contest over who would be patron of the city of Athens.

THE BIRTH OF SCIENCE

Ancient Science and Philosophy

SCIENCE HAS ITS ROOTS IN GREECE MORE THAN 2,000 YEARS AGO. HOWEVER THE WAY THE GREEK THINKERS INVESTIGATED THE WORLD WAS VERY DIFFERENT TO THE WAY SCIENTISTS DO TODAY.

A WORLD OF LEARNING

THE ANCIENT GREEKS CAME UP WITH MANY THEORIES ABOUT THE WORLD THEY LIVED IN. BUT THEY DID NOT CARRY OUT EXPERIMENTS TO FIND OUT WHICH THEORIES WERE CORRECT, AS SCIENTISTS DO TODAY.

Instead, they preferred to spend their time discussing their ideas. Today, we know that most of the ideas that the ancient Greeks had about the world were in fact wrong. However, their basic approach was that the Universe is controlled by underlying rules that people are able to understand. And this fundamental principle is the key to the way that science has been studied ever since.

▼ *The great library at Alexandria in Egypt was built and opened by Ptolemy in about 300 BCE. It was intended to house all the world's knowledge, and contained many Greek writings.*

THE SPREAD OF SCIENCE

In 149 BCE, the Roman Empire controlled Greece. Scientific development slowed, but the Romans spread the Greek discoveries through Europe. When the Roman Empire collapsed in 476 CE, a 'Dark Age' began in Europe, with almost no scientific progress. However, in the Middle East, scientific writings from Greece and India were translated and inspired new discoveries. China and India had been developing their own scientific expertise for centuries.

▲ This wall-painting by the Italian painter Raphael shows the School of Athens, an academy set up by the great Greek philosopher Plato.

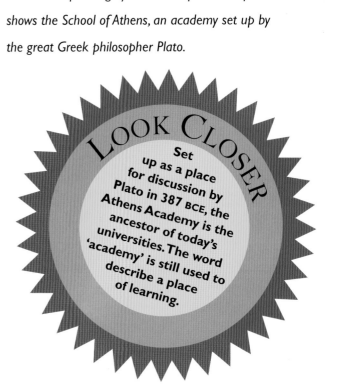

LOOK CLOSER

Set up as a place for discussion by Plato in 387 BCE, the Athens Academy is the ancestor of today's universities. The word 'academy' is still used to describe a place of learning.

PYTHAGORAS

Pythagoras is famous for believing that 'everything is number'. He founded a sect with followers, now called the Pythagoreans, who were fascinated by numbers and by geometry — the science of shapes.

The Pythagoreans believed, correctly, that the Earth is a spinning sphere. But the sect was nothing like a team of scientists today — in fact, most of the Pythagoreans' beliefs were more like superstition than science. However, both the science and the superstition lasted. The sect became very powerful and was still in existence a century later. Its idea that numbers can be used to explain the Universe is also accepted by scientists today.

LOOK CLOSER

The Pythagoreans had some very odd rules. They ate no beans, forbade each other to sit on pots of a certain size, and would not allow swallows to nest under their roofs.

Pythagoras believed that all numbers could be expressed as ratios.

For instance, one quarter is the ratio of 1 to 4, which we write as $\frac{1}{4}$.

When a student called Hippasus proved this was not true for some numbers, he was executed!

▶ *Pythagoras realized that simple shapes such as triangles could be described in terms of numbers.*

◀ *Pythagoras found that strings plucked together, for example on a harp, will sound harmonious if their lengths are related to each other by certain numbers.*

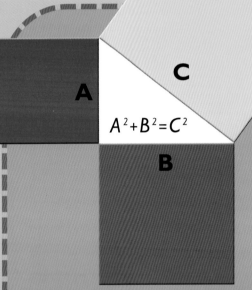

C

A

$A^2 + B^2 = C^2$

B

GREEK TRIANGLES

Pythagoras worked out that it is possible to calculate the length of any side of a right-angled triangle if the lengths of the other two sides are known. Adding together the squares of the two short sides gives the square of the length of the longest side. This theory, called Pythagoras' Theorem, contains the mathematical ideas of squares and square roots, which are key parts of mathematics today. Triangles fascinated the Pythagoreans. The sect described a particular triangle that had sides of equal length as 'the fount and root of ever-flowing nature'.

BCE
c.580   Born on the Greek island of Samos
c.560   Visits the philosopher Thales, who introduces him to mathematical ideas
c.550   Studies under Egyptian priests in Memphis, Egypt
c.530   Settles in Crotone, a Greek colony in Italy, and establishes a sect there
c.500   Flees persecution
c.490   Dies in the Greek city of Metapontium

ARISTOTLE

THE SON OF A PHYSICIAN, ARISTOTLE QUESTIONED THE WORLD AROUND HIM, TRYING TO WORK OUT WHY THINGS HAPPENED. ALTHOUGH MOST OF HIS CONCLUSIONS WERE WRONG, MANY WERE ACCEPTED FOR CENTURIES.

Aristotle was a philosopher who wrote about many branches of science, including physics, biology, medicine and earth sciences. His father was the personal physician of King Amyntas of Macedon, so the young boy was educated as a member of the aristocracy. When Aristotle was 18, he was sent to Athens to study under the great philosopher Plato, at his Academy. Plato recognized him as his brightest pupil, and in later life Aristotle became one of the most influential teachers and philosophers of all time.

▲ *This elaborate Roman mosaic shows the philosopher Plato at the Academy in Athens. Plato is shown seated under the tree in the centre, surrounded by some of his many pupils, including Aristotle.*

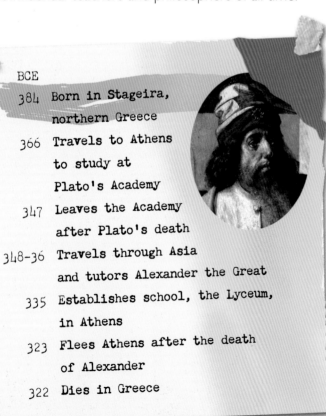

BCE
384 Born in Stageira, northern Greece
366 Travels to Athens to study at Plato's Academy
347 Leaves the Academy after Plato's death
348-36 Travels through Asia and tutors Alexander the Great
335 Establishes school, the Lyceum, in Athens
323 Flees Athens after the death of Alexander
322 Dies in Greece

Aristotle founded his school, the Lyceum, in 335 BCE and ran it for 12 years.

His favourite pupil at the Lyceum was Theophrastus, whose main interest was botany.

After Aristotle's death, his original manuscripts became the property of Theophrastus.

LOOK CLOSER

The students at Aristotle's school, the Lyceum, became known by everyone as 'peripatetics' because they copied Aristotle's habit of 'strolling about' as he taught them.

ARISTOTLE AND ALEXANDER

After he left Plato's Academy, Aristotle travelled through Asia before marrying Hermias of Atarneus' daughter, with whom he had a daughter called Pythias. In about 343 BCE, he was invited by King Philip II of Macedon to become tutor to his young son, Alexander. For several years, Aristotle trained the future Alexander the Great in rhetoric and literature, science, medicine and philosophy. His gift to Alexander, a copy of the Iliad, was one of the young king's most prized possessions. Alexander is said to have slept with the book under his pillow – along with his dagger.

▼ Aristotle (below right) tutors the young Alexander at the court of Philip II of Macedon.

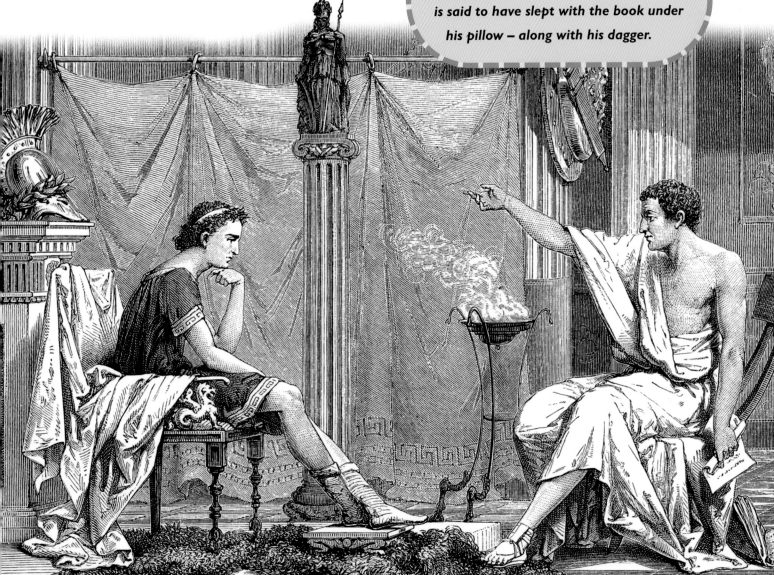

ARCHIMEDES

ARCHIMEDES WAS NOT ONLY ONE OF THE GREATEST MATHEMATICIANS WHO EVER LIVED, HE WAS AN INVENTOR AS WELL. HE LIVED IN SYRACUSE, SICILY.

Syracuse was at war with Rome for many years. Archimedes helped defend his city from attacking ships by inventing machines that dragged the ships from the water or sank them by hurling stones at them.

Finally the Romans won, breaking through the city walls while most of the guards were celebrating a feast day. Marcellus, the leader of the Romans, wanted Archimedes captured alive. However, when a soldier found the scientist, Archimedes was busily working out a maths problem in the sand. Archimedes waved the Roman away, and the soldier killed him.

Archimedes is supposed to have set fire to Roman ships by concentrating sunlight on them.

Most people thought this was impossible, until experiments took place in 1747.

That year, his method was tried again - and set both ships and houses alight.

LOOK CLOSER

Archimedes worked out that the number of sand grains that would fill the Universe was a thousand trillion trillion trillion trillion trillion (one followed by 63 noughts!).

▶ It is said that Archimedes discovered his famous principle (see box right) when he saw his bath overflowing – and ran naked down the street shouting 'Eureka!' ('I have found it!').

BCE

287 Born in Syracuse, Sicily

275 Syracuse taken over by King Hiero II, Archimedes' friend

c.269 Goes to study in Alexandria, Egypt; hears about or invents the Archimedean Screw water-pump, still in use today

c.265 Solves the golden crown problem

c.263 Returns to Syracuse

c.215 Hiero II dies

214 Siege of Syracuse begins

213 Roman attack repelled by 'Archimedes' heat ray'

212 Archimedes killed by Roman soldier

ARCHIMEDES' PRINCIPLE

Above is one of the machines that Archimedes invented to protect his city. But not all his discoveries were so warlike. King Hiero wanted to find out if his crown was made of solid gold. Archimedes dunked the crown in water, measuring the amount that overflowed. Then he did the same with a lump of pure gold of the same weight as the crown. He found that less water overflowed, so the pure gold must have taken up less space than the crown. This proved that the crown must be made partly of a lighter material, and the king had been cheated. Archimedes had shown that an object in a liquid is pressed upwards by a force that is equal to the weight of the liquid it pushes out of the way. This is Archimedes' principle.

ZHANG HENG

ZHANG HENG COMBINED HIS LOVE OF POETRY WITH A FASCINATION WITH SCIENCE, ESPECIALLY ASTRONOMY.

After studying at university and working as a minor civil servant, at the age of 34, Zhang Heng was summoned to the court of Emperor An in Luoyang, the Chinese capital city of the Han dynasty. Emperor An had heard of Zhang's great skills in mathematics, and soon he had become a member of the court. Zhang was eventually promoted to become an advisor to the next emperor, Shun. Zhang Heng divided his time between protecting Shun from court intrigues, studying science and writing poetry.

TIME IN ANCIENT CHINA

Zhang lived long before mechanical clocks were invented. Instead, time was often measured by a water clock – a container out of which water flowed slowly. The more water that flowed, the more time had passed. However, as the amount of water in the container decreased, the flow gradually slowed down, so the clocks were very inaccurate. Zhang invented a water clock with an extra tank that kept the flow constant. As Chief Astronomer, Zhang had many duties connected with time, including predicting lucky and unlucky days.

▲ *Zhang may have invented this distance-measuring device. After it had travelled a certain distance, a mechanical wooden figure struck a drum. After it had gone ten times as far, another wooden figure struck a gong or a bell.*

When an earthquake happened, a pendulum probably swung inside the earthquake detector.

It released a ball from the mouth of a dragon and it fell into the mouth of a frog.

◀ *This is a replica of Zhang's earthquake detector. One day, it registered that an earthquake had taken place, although no one at court felt it. Many people mocked Zhang – until a messenger arrived to report an earthquake over 400 km away, in the direction the detector had shown.*

STAR SPHERE

Zhang Heng built a bronze armillary sphere, which was a model of the night sky with the Earth at its centre. A system of water-powered gears moved the sphere to imitate the motion of the stars in the sky. Armillary spheres had been invented before Zhang's birth, but the one he developed (see the replica above) was the first to be powered by water.

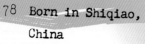
LOOK CLOSER

Zhang was put in charge of testing the literacy of people who wanted to work for Emperor An. They each had to know at least 9,000 different Chinese characters.

AVICENNA

AVICENNA WAS KNOWN AS 'THE PRINCE OF PHYSICIANS' BECAUSE OF HIS GREAT MEDICAL SKILL. HE BECAME AN EXCELLENT DOCTOR PARTLY BY STUDYING EVERYTHING THAT WAS KNOWN AT THE TIME ABOUT MEDICINE.

However, unlike most of his colleagues, Avicenna did not believe everything that he read. He also studied the illnesses carefully, finding out for himself the best way to treat his patients.

Avicenna was not only a physician, he was also an astronomer, physicist, mathematician and chemist. He was a deeply religious man, who tried to combine his knowledge of science and religion to work out both the secrets of the Universe and the best ways to organize people and nations.

▼ *This picture shows three great physicians from different times. Galen (130–200 CE), sits on the left, with Avicenna in the centre and Hippocrates (c. 460–370 BCE) on the right. All of them influenced medicine for centuries after their deaths.*

GALENVS · AVICENA · VPOCRATES

980	Born in Khurmaithan, near Bukhara in what is now Uzbekistan
996	Begins to practise medicine
997	Cures Emir Nuh ibn Mansur of a dangerous illness
998	Becomes physician at the court of the Emir
1025	His medical encyclopedia, *The Canon of Medicine*, is completed
1037	Dies, perhaps by poison, in Hamadan, northern Persia (now Iran)
1593	An Arabic text of *The Canon of Medicine* is published in Rome

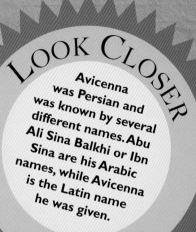

LOOK CLOSER

Avicenna was Persian and was known by several different names. Abu Ali Sina Balkhi or Ibn Sina are his Arabic names, while Avicenna is the Latin name he was given.

◄ The picture shows Avicenna and other physicians being consulted by someone suffering from smallpox (on the right). Because Avicenna worked hard to observe the exact symptoms of illnesses, he was able to discover that smallpox and measles are different diseases.

Avicenna's involvement in politics led to all sorts of problems for him.

He was imprisoned on several occasions, but managed to escape each time.

It is possible that he may have been assassinated for political reasons.

THE CANON OF MEDICINE

This is an illustration from Avicenna's masterpiece, The Canon of Medicine, in which he brought together all that was known about medicine. It filled 14 volumes and was the standard textbook in the Middle East and Europe until the 17th century. The illustration is very inaccurate because the cutting open of dead bodies was not allowed. People had to work out how the body worked by studying animals.

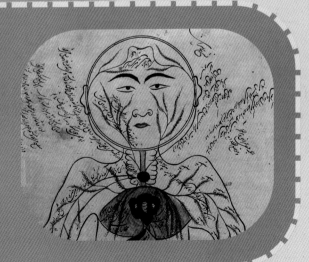

The Danish astronomer Tycho Brahe sits in his observatory on the island of Hven. Some men are observing the stars (top), while others (below) record their observations.

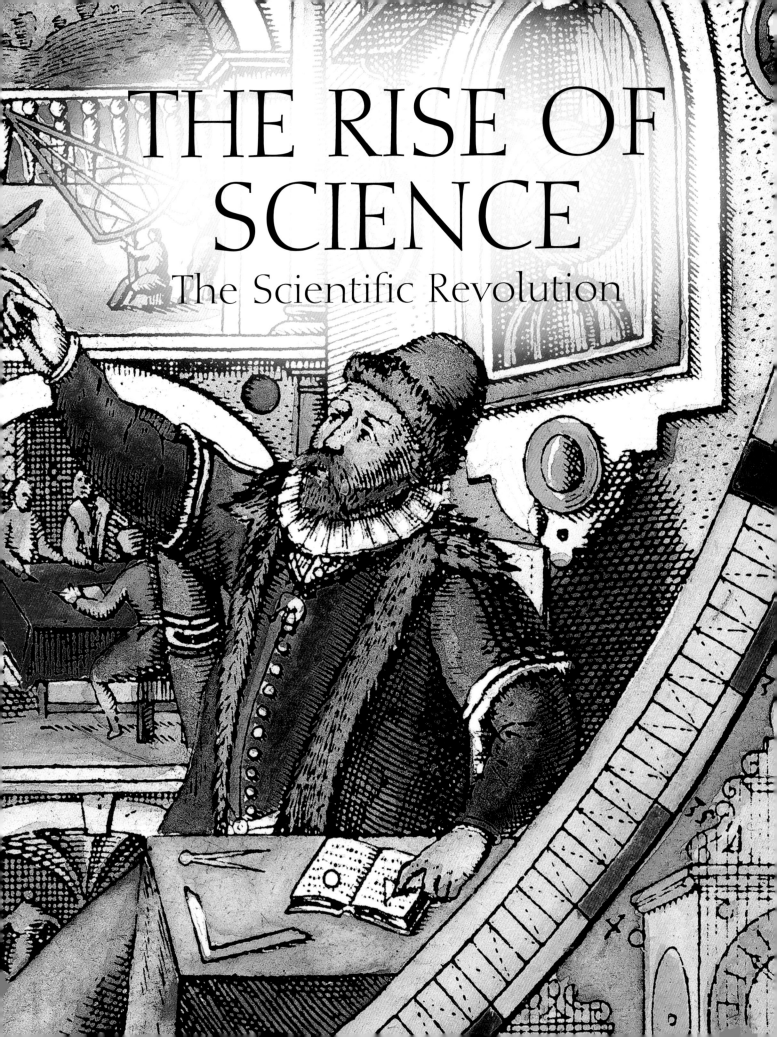

THE RISE OF SCIENCE

SCIENCE

The Scientific Revolution

IN EUROPE

IN THE 1500S,

A PERIOD CALLED THE

SCIENTIFIC

REVOLUTION BEGAN.

EUROPEAN SCIENTISTS

GRADUALLY REJECTED

THE IDEAS OF

THE ANCIENT GREEKS

FOR THEORIES

THAT WERE BASED

ON EXPERIMENTS.

A REVOLUTION IN SCIENCE

FROM ABOUT 146 BCE, WHEN GREECE WAS TAKEN OVER BY THE ROMAN EMPIRE, SCIENTIFIC PROGRESS IN EUROPE WAS SLOW.

Most science consisted only of discussing the ideas of the Greek philosophers, although there were some new discoveries elsewhere in the world. The situation began to change in the 1500s.

The Scientific Revolution in Europe established mathematics as an important part of science. Scientists also developed scientific methods, using observation and experiment.

▼ *It was in bustling European cities such as Verona in Italy, shown here in this hand-coloured woodcut, that the Scientific Revolution took place.*

In 1543, anatomist Andreas Vesalius published *The Workings of the Human Body.*

Until then, doctors had used centuries-old writings based on the study of animals.

◄ Alchemists tried to find ways to live forever, with equipment that is still used in modern chemistry.

THE PRINTING REVOLUTION

The Scientific Revolution was helped by new technology. In about 1439, in Germany, Johann Gutenberg invented a new type of printing press, which meant that books could be made quickly and cheaply. Before this, books had been copied by hand, which was very slow and meant that many errors were introduced. Gutenberg's press used print blocks with moveable letters. Scientific knowledge could now be communicated more quickly and easily than ever before.

NICOLAUS COPERNICUS

UNTIL THE 1500S, MOST PEOPLE THOUGHT THE EARTH WAS THE CENTRE OF THE UNIVERSE. COPERNICUS THOUGHT DIFFERENTLY, BELIEVING THAT THE EARTH AND THE OTHER PLANETS WENT AROUND THE SUN.

Copernicus studied law, medicine and mathematics as well as astronomy. He explained his theories about the Universe in a book, *On the Revolution of the Celestial Spheres*. But he did not publish the book until the very end of his life because he was afraid of criticism. It was over a century before most scientists accepted Copernicus' theory.

LOOK CLOSER

Copernicus' study of medicine led to his invention of a potion that he thought would cure every illness. The mixture included beetles, silver, sapphire, bones and the heart of a deer.

1473   Born in Torun, Poland

1491–   Attends Krakow
1495   University where he begins to study astronomy

1496   Studies law in Bologna, Italy

1501   Studies medicine at Padua, Italy

1514   Puts forward his idea about the Earth going round the Sun, but only in letters to friends

1526   Assists with mapping Poland

1543   *On the Revolution of the Celestial Spheres* is published; dies in Frombork, Poland

▼ Copernicus studied mathematics at the University of Krakow, in Poland. This statue, showing him holding a model of the Solar System with the Sun at the centre, is in Krakow.

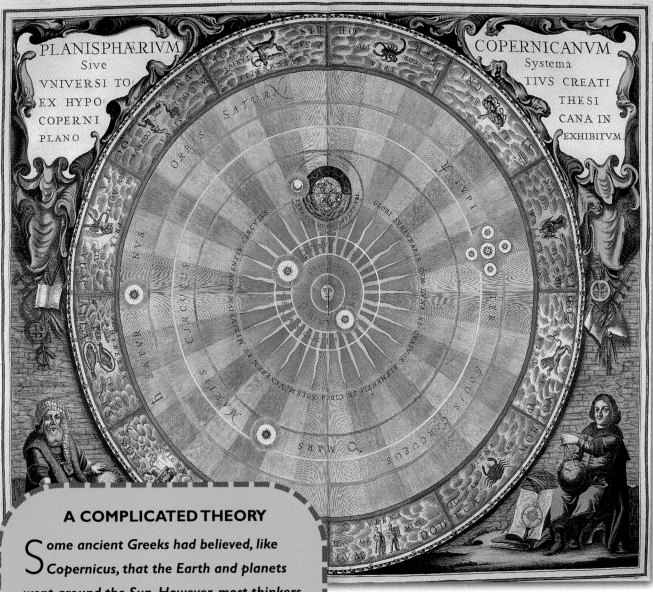

▲ This is the Solar System according to Copernicus, with the Sun at the centre, and the Earth, Moon and the other known planets circling around it.

A COMPLICATED THEORY

Some ancient Greeks had believed, like Copernicus, that the Earth and planets went around the Sun. However, most thinkers followed Aristotle's teachings that the Sun and planets went around the Earth. Even Copernicus did not understand that the planets move in elliptical (oval) orbits. He thought, like all the other scientists of the time, that the planets moved in small circles that were attached to larger circles. This meant that his 'Heliocentric' (Sun-centred) theory ended up being more complicated than the 'Geocentric' (Earth-centred) theory that it was intended to replace.

After Copernicus' book was published, there were many arguments about its truth.

The Catholic church decided that Copernicus was wrong, and banned his book until 1835.

WILLIAM GILBERT

HE WORKED FOR ELIZABETH I AND JAMES I OF ENGLAND AS THEIR PERSONAL DOCTOR. BUT WILLIAM GILBERT IS REALLY FAMOUS FOR HIS DISCOVERY THAT THE EARTH IS A HUGE MAGNET. AFTER HIM, NO BREAKTHROUGHS IN MAGNETISM WERE MADE UNTIL THE 1820S.

Until Gilbert's time, the only magnets that had been identified were lodestones, pieces of rock made of naturally occuring magnetic material. Gilbert discovered how to make new magnets. He also found out how to destroy the magnetic power of magnets. He did this by heating them up.

LOOK CLOSER

At this time, scientific discoveries were thought of as entertaining rather than useful. Centuries later, the world was changed by inventions using electricity and magnetism.

▼ Gilbert explained his discoveries to Elizabeth I. Here, he shows how static electricity can make feathers stick to an amber rod. The rod is first 'charged' by rubbing it with fur.

THE MAGNETIC EARTH

The discovery that the Earth is a magnet explained why compasses point towards the north and south poles. Compass needles are small magnets that line themselves up with other magnets, including the Earth. The Earth's magnetic field is caused by the motion of liquid metal deep inside the planet, and it extends out into space. When particles from the Sun encounter it, colourful glows of light called aurorae appear. They are brightest near the poles, where the magnetic field is strongest.

▲ *This is an illustration from Gilbert's book,* On the Magnet. *It shows that an iron rod can be magnetized by lining it up in a north-south direction and hammering it.*

Gilbert wrote his book in English – most scientific books were in Latin.

The book became famous and was soon translated into many other languages.

1544 Born in Colchester, England

1569 Awarded medical doctorate after studying at Cambridge University

1573 Moves to London and becomes a fellow of the Royal College of Physicians

1600 Publishes *On the Magnet: Magnetic Bodies and the Great Magnet Earth*

1601 Becomes Elizabeth I's personal doctor

1603 Dies of bubonic plague in London

TYCHO BRAHE

T HIS NOBLEMAN WAS ONE OF THE
MOST WEALTHY PEOPLE IN DENMARK.
BUT HE IS FAMOUS FOR HIS AMAZING
ASTRONOMICAL INVENTIONS AND DISCOVERIES.

Tyge (known as Tycho) Ottersen Brahe de Knudstrup
was born at his family's ancestral seat, Knutstorp Castle,
on 14 December, 1546. He had a twin brother, who did
not survive, and two sisters. When he was two years old
his uncle, Jorgen Brahe, took him away from his family to
live with him at Tostrup Castle. Jorgen brought up his
nephew as if he was his only son.

In 1559, Brahe began law studies at the University
of Copenhagen. It was there, on 21 August, 1560, that
he saw his first eclipse of the Sun. This event
so fascinated him that he began
a series of investigations and
observations that he would
continue for the rest
of his life.

1546	Born in Denmark
1548	Begins life with uncle Jorgen
1559	Attends University of Copenhagen
1566	Loses part of nose in a duel
1572	Identifies a supernova in the constellation Cassiopeia
1576–81	Two observatories built for Brahe on the island of Hven
1583	Birth of Kirstine, the first of his eight children
1601	Dies from a bladder infection.

► *King*
Frederick of
Denmark gave Brahe
an estate on the island
of Hven to build an
observatory. Brahe
can be seen bottom
right using one of his
inventions, an enormous quadrant.

Tycho Brahe was the last great astronomer to work without a telescope. His observations were meticulous, and probably the most accurate ever made by an astronomer.

Brahe kept a tame elk on Hven. It roamed freely throughout the castle and grounds.

▲ On 11 November, 1572, Tycho was watching the stars from Herrevad Abbey and noticed a very bright star in the constellation Cassiopeia (above). He had discovered a supernova, now called SN 1572.

The elk died after becoming drunk on beer, falling downstairs and breaking a leg!

BRAHE'S PRECIOUS NOSE

While he was a student, Tycho Brahe lost part of the bridge of his nose in a drunken duel with another student, Manderup Parsbjerg, possibly over who was the better mathematician. Tycho wore a false nose for the rest of his life. This was said to be made from a blend of gold and silver, held in place with a sticky ointment! His tomb was opened in 1901 and his remains examined by experts. They found traces of green round the nose – a sign that it had been exposed to copper, rather than silver or gold.

GALILEO GALILEI

GALILEO GALILEI WAS A SCIENTIFIC GENIUS. WHEN HE HEARD ONLY A VAGUE DESCRIPTION OF THE FIRST TELESCOPE, HE QUICKLY BUILT HIS OWN AND USED IT TO STUDY THE NIGHT SKY.

As a result, Galileo found out that the Moon has valleys and mountains. He also saw that the Milky Way is made of stars and discovered four of Jupiter's moons.

These breakthroughs would have been enough to make Galileo famous, but he did much more. He worked out the scientific laws that describe how the speeds of objects change as they fall or swing from side to side. This eventually led him to the invention of the pendulum clock.

LOOK CLOSER

Galileo developed a version of today's pocket calculators. It could work out how to aim cannons and how much gunpowder to put in them. He called this invention a 'military compass'.

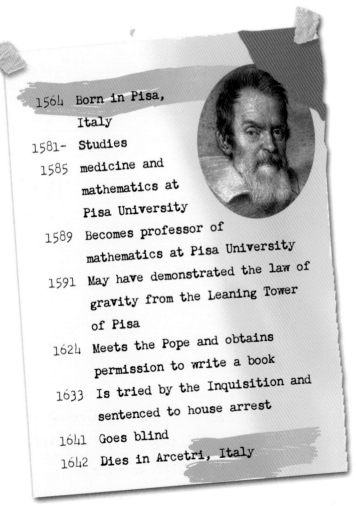

1564 Born in Pisa, Italy

1581– Studies
1585 medicine and mathematics at Pisa University

1589 Becomes professor of mathematics at Pisa University

1591 May have demonstrated the law of gravity from the Leaning Tower of Pisa

1624 Meets the Pope and obtains permission to write a book

1633 Is tried by the Inquisition and sentenced to house arrest

1641 Goes blind

1642 Dies in Arcetri, Italy

Galileo offered to show priests the moons of Jupiter through his telescope.

The priests were unwilling to look, because they had decided the moons could not exist.

MOUNTAINS OF THE MOON

Until Galileo, scientists thought that the Moon was perfectly smooth and spherical – because Aristotle had said so. Galileo's discovery of mountains on the Moon showed that it was not a perfect sphere. To support Aristotle, it was claimed that there was an invisible smooth layer above the mountains. In answer, Galileo suggested that the layer had invisible mountains on it!

◀ This imaginary scene shows one priest using Galileo's telescope to look at the Moon, while Galileo shows his drawings of the Moon to another.

Galileo used his observations and experiments to find out how the world worked. He used maths as well as arguments to explain his theories.

Throughout his life, Galileo's approach – and his personality – involved him in many arguments, and put his life in danger. He wanted to write a book about the question of whether or not the Earth went around the Sun. He knew that this was a sensitive issue, so he obtained permission from the Pope on the condition that arguments were given both for and against the idea. When the book was published, Galileo's conclusion was obvious: the Earth *does* go around the Sun. The Pope was furious, and summoned Galileo to Rome to explain himself. He narrowly avoided being tortured, was forced to deny his theory, forbidden to discuss it again and sentenced to house arrest. But Galileo kept working until he died, developing new areas of science even after he became blind. He was the first successful modern scientist.

In 1971, a feather and hammer were dropped and landed at the same time on the airless Moon.

Galileo was right - without air resistance, objects of different weights fall at the same speed!

▼ *Galileo was put on trial by the Inquisition in the Vatican in Rome, 1633, and found 'vehemently suspect of heresy'.*

A SCIENTIFIC PLAY

The book that caused Galileo so much trouble was written as a sort of play with three characters. One believes the Earth goes round the Sun, one disagrees and the other is neutral. The main proof that Galileo gives that the Earth is in motion is that otherwise there would be no tides. This is wrong, but a lot of the other science in the book is correct. The Pope was annoyed that the book came down on the side of the Sun-centred theory. He also thought the simple-minded character, Simplicio, who believes in the Earth-centred theory, was actually modelled on him!

▲ In old age at his house in Arcetri, the blind Galileo relied on help from various people, including a secretary and his son Vincenzio, to write his books and get them published.

▶ In 1995, after a six-year journey, a space probe arrived at Jupiter to study the planet and the moons that Galileo had discovered nearly four centuries earlier. The space probe was called Galileo, too.

JOHANNES KEPLER

DETERMINED TO SOLVE THE PROBLEM THAT HAD PUZZLED ASTRONOMERS BEFORE HIM, KEPLER TACKLED THE QUESTION 'HOW DO THE PLANETS MOVE?'

Burdened with terrible eyesight, many illnesses, poverty and a vast mass of planetary data, the task took him eight years. Finally, he discovered that the paths of the planets around the Sun are elliptical (oval) in shape. He went on to work out the laws that describe the way they speed up and slow down as they move. To make money, Kepler made his living partly by fortune-telling, and he wrote one of the first science-fiction stories – about a trip to the Moon.

LOOK CLOSER

Kepler's eyes were damaged by the smallpox when he was a child. In later life, he studied the way that human eyes work. He discovered the reasons for short- and long-sightedness.

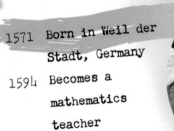

1571 Born in Weil der Stadt, Germany

1594 Becomes a mathematics teacher

1601 Obtains Tycho Brahe's data on the motion of the planets

1609 Publishes *A New Astronomy*, including two laws of planetary motion

1611 Explains the shape of honeycombs

1619 Publishes *The Harmony of the Worlds*, containing a third law of planetary motion

1630 Dies of a fever in Regensburg, Germany

Many people believed in witchcraft, and Kepler's mother was tried as a witch.

Kepler stopped all his scientific work until his mother's release in 1621.

◀ Witches were feared at this time. They were thought to have magical powers, to be servants of the Devil and to be helped by spirits in the forms of animals.

PATTERNS IN THE SKY

Compared to the stars, the planets change position in the sky from one night to the next. This picture tracks the movement of the planet Mars across the sky during a period of about one month. Kepler used patterns like this to work out the shape of the orbit of Mars around the Sun. He went on to work out the orbits of the five other known planets.

◀ Kepler was Holy Roman Emperor Rudolph II's court mathematician, a job that consisted mainly of casting Rudolph's horoscope.

WILLIAM HARVEY

F OR CENTURIES, SCIENTISTS HAD ACCEPTED THE THEORY OF GALEN, A ROMAN DOCTOR WHO LIVED IN THE 2ND CENTURY, THAT BLOOD IS FORMED IN THE LIVER AND DESTROYED IN THE BODY.

But William Harvey thought that science should be based on experiments, not ancient writings. His studies convinced him that blood circulated around the body over and over again, pumped on its journey by the heart. He also believed that mammals begin life as eggs, and Charles I let him dissect deer from his park to investigate this idea. However the eggs were too small to find, and he was not proved right until centuries after his death.

1578   Born in Folkestone, England

1539–1599   Studies medicine at Cambridge University, England

1599–1602   Studies medicine at Padua University, Italy

1616   First lecture on his theory of the circulation of the blood

1618   Becomes physician to James I

1625   Becomes physician to Charles I

1628   Publishes his theory

1636   Travels to Germany and Italy as diplomat for Charles I

1657   Dies in Roehampton, England

▲ Harvey worked as a physician to the English king Charles I. In this later portrait by Robert Hannah, Harvey is using a deer's heart to demonstrate his theory of blood circulation to the king.

Harvey was sure veins must be connected to arteries by blood vessels too small to see.

Using a microscope, Italian biologist Malpighi found these vessels after Harvey's death.

HARVEY AND THE WITCHES

In the 17th century, many innocent people were executed for witchcraft. People tried as witches were searched for nipple-shaped 'witch's marks', supposedly made by the devil. In 1633, a boy claimed that several people he knew were witches, and that he had seen them change into dogs and horses. Charles I sent four of these suspected witches to Harvey to be examined for marks. Harvey found the marks on one of them. Unusually for a doctor of the time, he argued that they were due to natural causes, and as a result, some of the women were released.

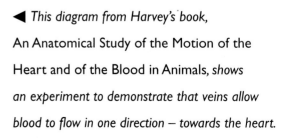

◄ This diagram from Harvey's book, An Anatomical Study of the Motion of the Heart and of the Blood in Animals, *shows an experiment to demonstrate that veins allow blood to flow in one direction – towards the heart.*

Energetic discussions and exchanges of scientific ideas took place in coffee houses all over Europe during the 17th and 18th centuries.

THE POWER OF SCIENCE

The Age of Reason

ELEGANT SCIENCE

THIS PERIOD IN HISTORY IS SOMETIMES KNOWN AS THE ENLIGHTENMENT. IT WAS A TIME WHEN MANY PEOPLE BELIEVED THAT HUMAN REASON COULD EXPLAIN HOW THE WORLD WORKED.

DURING THE 17TH AND 18TH CENTURIES, SCIENTISTS DEVELOPED POWERFUL NEW WAYS IN WHICH TO UNDERSTAND THE WORLD ABOUT THEM.

Scientists right across Europe developed new and wide-ranging theories. These theories began to explain the way all objects in space move, as well as the structure of the whole universe. The scientists began to delve into the relationships between all plants and animals, and to describe the laws that all matter obeys. This progress, during the period known as the Enlightenment, happened partly because the Church was not as opposed to scientific enquiry as it had been, so did not stand in its way.

▼ *The greatest scientist of the time was Isaac Newton, shown here in a painting by William Blake. Newton insisted that only theories that could be proved or disproved had any value. This soon became a key principle of science, and remains so today.*

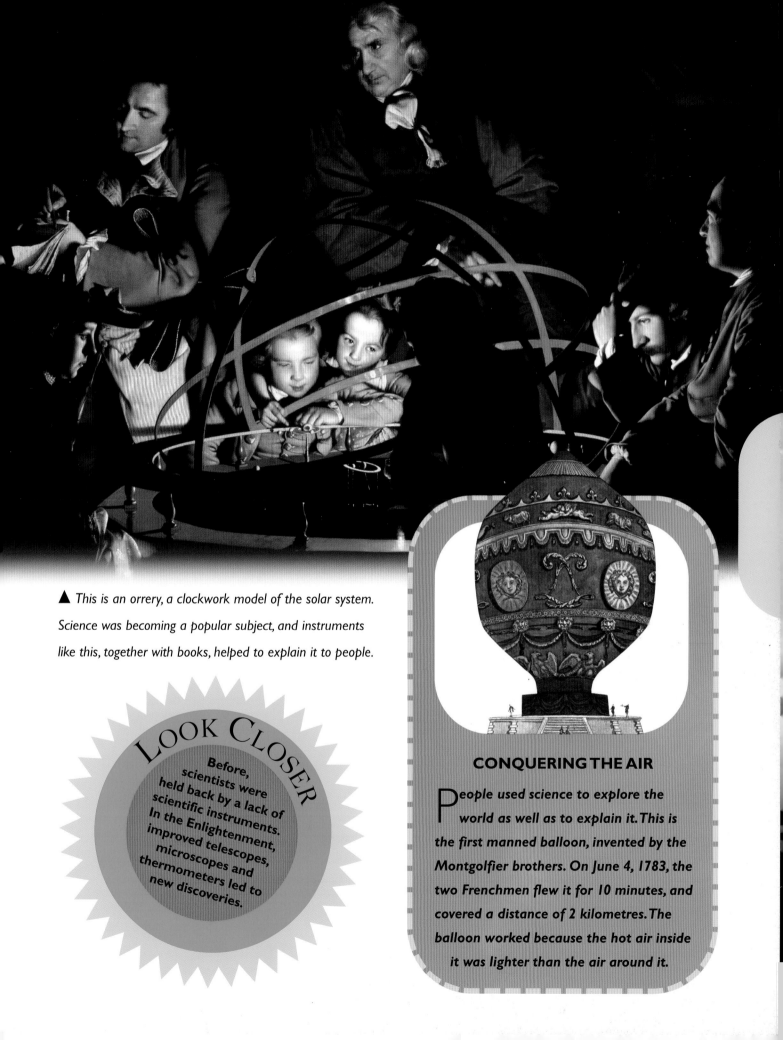

▲ This is an orrery, a clockwork model of the solar system. Science was becoming a popular subject, and instruments like this, together with books, helped to explain it to people.

LOOK CLOSER

Before, scientists were held back by a lack of scientific instruments. In the Enlightenment, improved telescopes, microscopes and thermometers led to new discoveries.

CONQUERING THE AIR

People used science to explore the world as well as to explain it. This is the first manned balloon, invented by the Montgolfier brothers. On June 4, 1783, the two Frenchmen flew it for 10 minutes, and covered a distance of 2 kilometres. The balloon worked because the hot air inside it was lighter than the air around it.

CHRISTIAAN HUYGENS

HUYGENS WORKED IN MANY AREAS OF SCIENCE. HE WAS FASCINATED BY THE NATURE OF LIGHT AND MADE VERY ACCURATE LENSES, WHICH HE USED TO BUILD A TELESCOPE.

Huygens was able to extend Galileo's discoveries about the planets with the observations he made with this telescope. He was an expert in mathematics, and used it as a powerful research tool, calculating the distance from Earth to a star. He also designed the first accurate clock using mathematics.

Huygens decided that all the planets in the Solar System were inhabited, and that the creatures that lived on Jupiter and Saturn had sailing ships!

THE SECRET OF LIGHT

Newton, who lived about the same time as Huygens, believed that light was made of fast-moving particles, like a hailstorm of tiny bullets. However, Huygens thought the way that light behaved could be more easily explained if it was made of waves. For most of the 18th century, Newton's theory was more popular, but the wave-theory replaced it at the beginning of the 19th century. In the early 20th century, scientists proved that light can behave like particles or waves. They also showed that when light behaves like a wave, it acts just as Huygens had described in his mathematical theories.

1629 Born in The Hague, in the Netherlands
1666 Works in the Academy of Sciences in Paris
1681 His Protestant religion makes him unpopular and he returns to The Hague
1655 Discovers the rings of Saturn and its largest moon, Titan
1658 Publishes *The Clock*
1663 Visits England and is elected a fellow of the Royal Society
1690 Publishes his *Treatise on Light*
1695 Dies in The Hague

▼ *Huygens can be seen here experimenting with a prism and a pendulum. His telescope is behind him, set up near the window, and a clock based on his design is on the wall.*

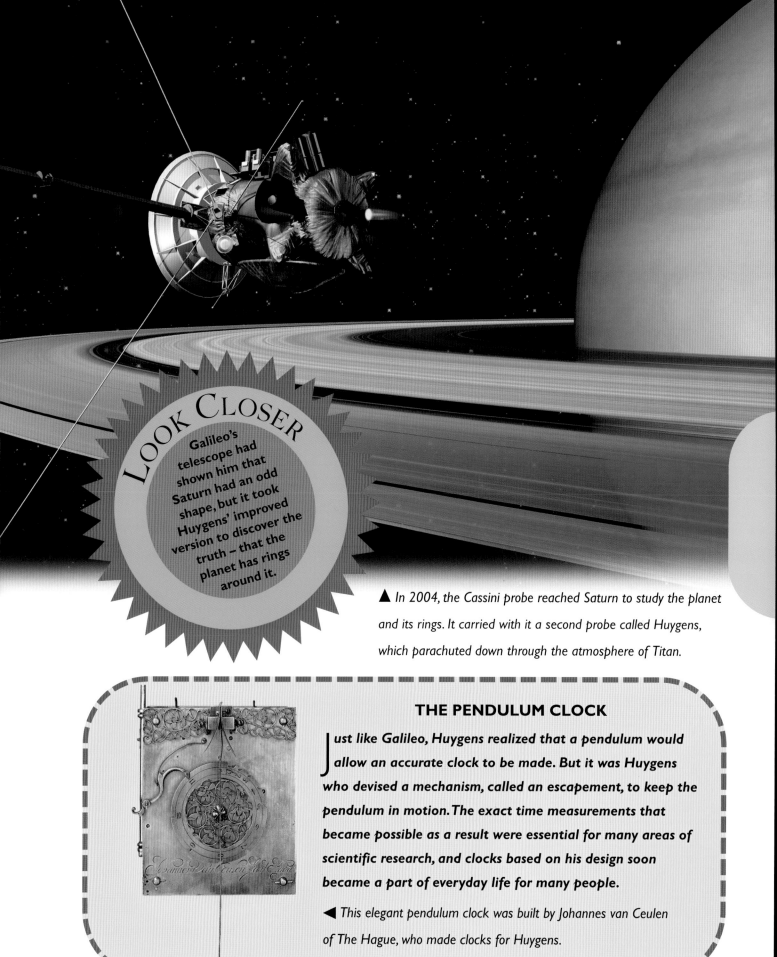

LOOK CLOSER

Galileo's telescope had shown him that Saturn had an odd shape, but it took Huygens' improved version to discover the truth – that the planet has rings around it.

▲ In 2004, the Cassini probe reached Saturn to study the planet and its rings. It carried with it a second probe called Huygens, which parachuted down through the atmosphere of Titan.

THE PENDULUM CLOCK

Just like Galileo, Huygens realized that a pendulum would allow an accurate clock to be made. But it was Huygens who devised a mechanism, called an escapement, to keep the pendulum in motion. The exact time measurements that became possible as a result were essential for many areas of scientific research, and clocks based on his design soon became a part of everyday life for many people.

◀ This elegant pendulum clock was built by Johannes van Ceulen of The Hague, who made clocks for Huygens.

ANTONI VAN LEEUWENHOEK

L EEUWENHOEK WAS A DRAPER, NOT A TRAINED SCIENTIST. HOWEVER, HE WAS FASCINATED BY THE AMAZING MINIATURE WORLDS THAT HE SAW THROUGH HIS MICROSCOPES.

These revealing instruments had been invented in about 1595 in Leeuwenhoek's native country, the Netherlands, but no-one used them quite as enthusiastically and productively as he did. Leeuwenhoek sent his discoveries to the English Royal Society in the form of illustrated letters. Soon many people were as excited as he was. They were intrigued by the tiny creatures and structures that existed all around them. With a microscope they could see them in rainwater, blood, mould and even in the grime from people's teeth!

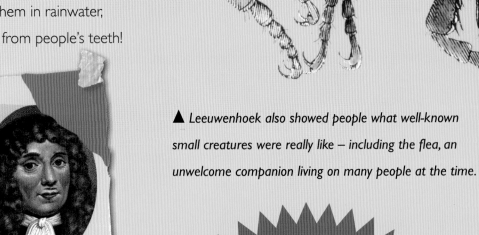

▲ *Leeuwenhoek also showed people what well-known small creatures were really like – including the flea, an unwelcome companion living on many people at the time.*

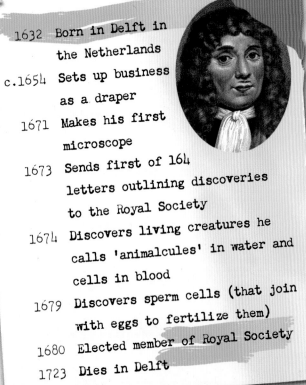

1632 Born in Delft in the Netherlands

c.1654 Sets up business as a draper

1671 Makes his first microscope

1673 Sends first of 164 letters outlining discoveries to the Royal Society

1674 Discovers living creatures he calls 'animalcules' in water and cells in blood

1679 Discovers sperm cells (that join with eggs to fertilize them)

1680 Elected member of Royal Society

1723 Dies in Delft

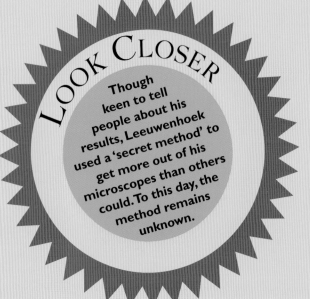

LOOK CLOSER

Though keen to tell people about his results, Leeuwenhoek used a 'secret method' to get more out of his microscopes than others could. To this day, the method remains unknown.

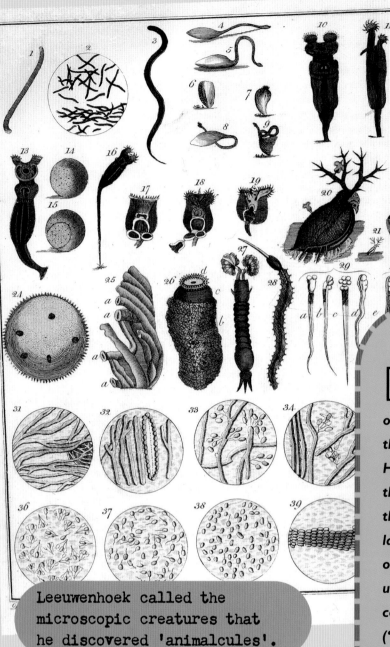

◄ *Here are Leeuwenhoek's drawings of some of the things he discovered. They included blood cells, sperm cells and many types of creatures with only a single cell, some of which he called 'cavorting beasties'.*

THE MICROSCOPES

During his working life, Leeuwenhoek made more than 400 microscopes, of which only nine survive. The key to their success was his skill as a lens-maker. He made at least 500 lenses, some of them as small as pinheads, and others that made things appear up to 275 times larger than life. His microscopes had just one tiny lens each, unlike today's, which use many lenses. The word microscope comes from the Greek words micron ('small'), and skopein ('to look at').

Leeuwenhoek called the microscopic creatures that he discovered 'animalcules'.

He calculated that there were about a million animalcules in a single drop of water.

Peter the Great of Russia and Queen Mary II of England came to see the animalcules.

ISAAC NEWTON

NEWTON IS POSSIBLY THE GREATEST SCIENTIST EVER, MAKING WORLD-CHANGING BREAKTHROUGHS IN ASTRONOMY, PHYSICS AND MATHEMATICS.

However, he was not always convinced that science mattered much – and he was at least as interested in alchemy. Perhaps the most surprising thing of all is that Newton was very reluctant to publish any of his work . Of course, if Newton's theories had proved wrong, this would be no real surprise, but for the most part, they were correct.

LOOK CLOSER

Newton could be just a little bit absent-minded. He was once found boiling his watch with an egg in his hand! He also started a walk with a horse and ended up with just the bridle.

▼ *Newton, seen here experimenting, made important discoveries about the science of light. He showed that white light can be broken into, or made from, a rainbow of colours.*

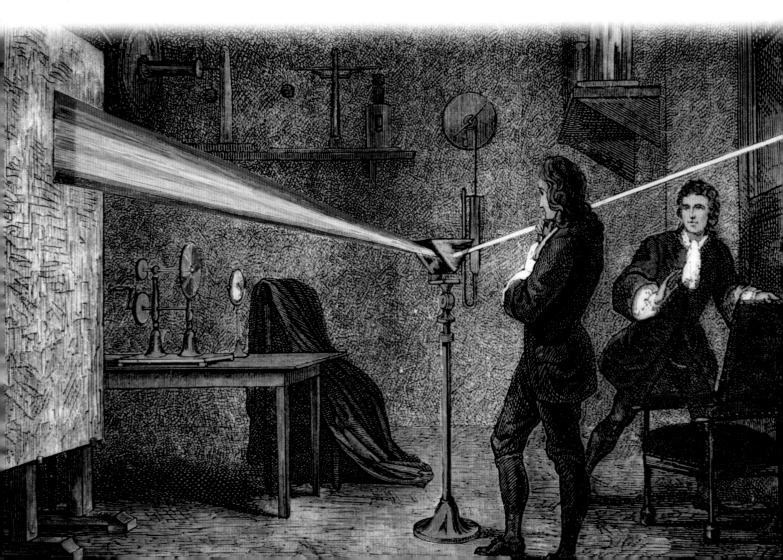

► *Newton was born in this manor house in Lincolnshire on Christmas Day, 1642. He was so tiny and weak that he was not expected to survive.*

Newton thought that no telescope that used a lens could ever work correctly.

He was wrong, but as a result he invented a mirror-based telescope that worked well.

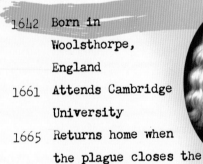

1642 Born in Woolsthorpe, England
1661 Attends Cambridge University
1665 Returns home when the plague closes the university
1671 Demonstrates reflecting telescope to the Royal Society
1687 Publishes Book 1 of *Mathematical Principles of Natural Philosophy*
1696 Becomes Warden of the Mint
1703 Becomes President of the Royal Society
1705 Is knighted
1727 Dies in London

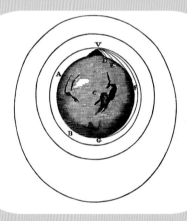

SPACE SCIENCE

Newton developed three laws of motion as well as a law of gravity. Applying a new sort of maths that he invented himself, he used the laws to explain the motion of objects in space. His diagram (above) shows that an object thrown hard enough sideways will orbit the Earth. Satellites and space stations behave just as Newton's theories predicted.

Newton's most important work, his theory of gravity, did not quite work because at the time no-one knew exactly how big the Earth was. Yet, when a new value for its size was found, Newton waited a very long time before bothering to check whether it proved him right – which it did. In his book *The Mathematical Principles of Natural Philosophy*, he says, 'I now demonstrate the frame of the system of the world.' And he does, showing how his equations of motion and gravity exactly predict the motion of the planets, the Moon and comets. Three centuries later, those same equations took people to the Moon.

▲ *It is said that Newton started to work out his theory of gravity when he saw an apple fall.*

▲ *Newton was a practical man as well as a great thinker. Not only did he construct this telescope, he also made the tools with which to build it.*

SECRETS AND FEUDS

Throughout his life, Isaac Newton was involved in many bitter arguments with other scientists – partly as a result of his secretive nature. He invented a branch of mathematics called calculus, which has been vital to science ever since, but he did not use it in his books. A German philosopher called Gottfried Leibniz came up with calculus too, and many arguments followed about who devised it first.

SCIENTIFIC DEBATE

Newton first joined and later took control of the scientific group in London called the Royal Society. Robert Hooke (above), who was an important scientist in his own right, was a fellow member, and the two men had many arguments over the years. One reason for this was that, even during this period, scientists often preferred arguments to experiments as a way of deciding which theories were correct.

In 1689, Newton was elected Member of Parliament for the University of Cambridge.

He sat in Parliament again in 1701-1702, but he was not a very memorable politician.

The only 'speech' he is known to have made was to ask for a window to be closed.

▼ Today's largest telescopes are based on Newton's design. Most of the objects they study move just as Newton's laws predict. This telescope, at La Palma in the Canary Islands, is named after him.

LOOK CLOSER

When he was only 26, Newton became a professor at Cambridge University. He spent a lot of his time there trying to work out the future of the world from statements in the Bible.

ANDERS CELSIUS

ALTHOUGH CELSIUS IS FAMOUS FOR THE TEMPERATURE SCALE THAT IS NAMED AFTER HIM, HE WORKED IN MANY OTHER AREAS OF SCIENCE, TOO.

In his home country of Sweden the northern lights (natural light displays in the sky) are often visible. Celsius wrote one of the first scientific studies of these lights. He also measured the brightnesses of stars, tried to work out how far away the Sun is and investigated the falling water level of the Baltic Sea.

His temperature scale, the basis for the one we use today, has two natural fixed points: the freezing and boiling points of pure water at normal air pressure. Celsius divided the difference between these points by 100 to give one degree centigrade.

1701	Born in Uppsala, Sweden
1723	Becomes secretary of the Uppsala Scientific Society
1731	Becomes Professor of Astronomy
1733	Publishes his work on the northern lights
1736	Takes part in the Lapland expedition
1740	Opens the observatory at Uppsala
1742	Proposes his temperature scale to the Swedish Academy of Sciences
1744	Dies in Uppsala of tuberculosis

▼ As water is heated, its molecules get more energy and move around more quickly, banging into one another harder. At boiling point, they break away from each other completely.

Newton had a theory that the Earth's spin causes it to flatten near the poles.

Celsius joined an expedition to the very north of Sweden - the 'Lapland expedition'.

The expedition measured the Earth's shape and proved that Newton's theory was correct.

CELSIUS CRATER ON THE MOON

Like many other famous scientists, Celsius has a crater on the Moon that is named after him. Most lunar craters were formed many millions of years ago, when meteorites crashed into the Moon and exploded on impact. Celsius is about 36 km across and located inside a larger, older crater. The surface of the Moon is scarred with millions of impact craters that can measure hundreds of kilometres across.

LOOK CLOSER

In the Celsius scale, the boiling point of water was 0 and the freezing point was 100. A few years after Celsius's death, Carl Linnaeus reversed the scale and that is the way we use it today.

▼ Celsius set up and managed Uppsala Astronomical Observatory. He equipped it with the latest instruments that he bought on journeys to France, Italy and Germany.

CARL LINNAEUS

BOTANIST AND EXPLORER LINNAEUS WAS THE FIRST PERSON TO DEVISE A SIMPLE AND PRACTICAL SYSTEM FOR NAMING ALL LIVING THINGS. THIS NAMING SYSTEM IS STILL IN USE TODAY.

Linnaeus was born on 23, May 1707 in the town of Stenbrohult, southern Sweden. His father was a pastor and an avid gardener. From 1727, Carl pursued medical and botanical studies at various universities. All of these led to the publication in 1735 of the first edition of his classification of living things, the *Systema Naturae*. In 1741, he was appointed to a professorship at Uppsala University, where he restored the botanical garden and inspired many students, including Daniel Solander.

After Linnaeus died, a collector sent his scientific work on a ship to England.

When the King of Sweden heard, he sent a ship to recover the collection for Sweden.

The collector's ship escaped, and the collection has been in London ever since.

◀ This illustrated page comes from Linnaeus' book about classification, Systema Naturae, *which began life as a slim pamphlet but grew into many volumes.*

▶ Linnaeus' botanical garden in Uppsala University is maintained as it was in his lifetime, with the plants arranged according to his system of classification.

THE *ENDEAVOUR* VOYAGE

Linnaeus' student Daniel Solander was one of the scientists who joined James Cook's first voyage to the Pacific Ocean on board the Endeavour (above). Solander was one of the botanists who coined the name Botanist Bay, which became Botany Bay.

1707 Born in Sweden

1727 Studies medicine and botany in various universities

1731 Mounts botanical expedition to Lapland to collect plants

1735 Publishes first edition of *Systema Naturae*

1741 Is appointed professor at Uppsala University

1758 Establishes a museum for his botanical collection at Hamarby

1761 Is given the title Carl von Linné

1778 Dies at Uppsala.

LOOK CLOSER

Linnaeus tried to grow plants to replace imports, so boosting the Swedish economy. Unfortunately, cacao, tea, coffee, bananas and rice were not successful in the cold Swedish climate.

WILLIAM AND CAROLINE HERSCHEL

As a young man, Frederick William Herschel (known as William) loved music and was an oboist in an army band. He also loved England, where he settled after a visit he made when he was just a teenager.

But Herschel's greatest love was astronomy. When his sister Caroline joined him in Bath, they began to build a telescope. Larger versions followed, and together the Herschels studied the night sky. Caroline discovered many new comets and nebulae, and William found five new worlds – the planet Uranus and two of its moons, as well as two moons of Saturn. He also made the first map of the whole universe of stars.

William tried to work out the shape of our Galaxy from his observations.

As they worked, he and Caroline catalogued some tiny cloudy areas.

William said they were galaxies. He was proved right 100 years later.

► *This is the Herschels' largest telescope, a 12 m iron tube with a mirror over 1 m wide. At least one astronomer fell off it in the dark and broke his arm.*

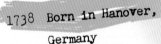

1738 Born in Hanover, Germany

1756 William moves to England

1757 Seven Years War breaks out

1781 Discovers the planet Uranus

1783 Discovers that the Sun is moving through space

1787 Discovers two moons of Uranus

1789 Discovers two moons of Saturn

1821 Is elected as President of the Royal Astronomical Society

1822 Dies, aged 84 (84 years on Earth equals 1 year on Uranus!)

INVISIBLE ASTRONOMY

William discovered that sunlight contains invisible heat-rays, now called infrared. Modern telescopes image the infrared light of the stars, planets and galaxies that the Herschels discovered.

▲ By discovering Uranus, the first new planet in thousands of years, William became rich and famous. He first called the planet 'George's Star' in honour of the English king.

LOOK CLOSER

Not all of William's ideas were correct. He thought sunspots were holes in a burning atmosphere through which the cool (and inhabited) surface of the Sun could be seen.

1750	Born in Hanover, Germany
1772	Moves to England
1783	Discovers three new nebulae
1786– 1797	Discovers eight comets
1796	Granted an annual salary by George III, becoming the first professional female scientist
1822	Returns to Hanover when William dies
1828	Awarded the Gold Medal of the Royal Astronomical Society for her catalogue of nebulae
1848	Dies in Hanover

ANTOINE LAVOISIER

THE FOUNDER OF MODERN CHEMISTRY, THE FRENCH NOBLEMAN ANTOINE-LAURENT DE LAVOISIER DISCOVERED THAT OXYGEN IN THE AIR WAS NEEDED FOR BREATHING AND BURNING. HE ALSO NAMED HYDROGEN AND HELPED ESTABLISH THE CHEMICAL NAMES USED TODAY.

Lavoisier was born to a wealthy family in Paris. At the age of only five, he inherited a large fortune when his mother died. As a student he studied chemistry, botany, astronomy and mathematics, but qualified in law. At the age of 25, he was elected to the French Academy of Sciences. In his work for the government as one of only 28 tax collectors, he developed the metric system – all this before being branded a traitor for this work. He was executed in 1794, at the height of the French Revolution.

1743 Born in Paris

1754-61 Studies law at the College Mazarin

1764 Publishes first scientific papers

1768 Is elected a member of the French Academy of Sciences

1769 Becomes a tax collector in the Ferme Générale

1771 Marries Marie-Anne Pierrette Paulze, who translated for him as well as illustrating his books

1787 Writes *Method of Chemical Nomenclature*

1794 Is beheaded during the French Revolution

◄ *Lavoisier and his wife worked closely together. She learned English so that she could translate material for him. She also drew sketches of his experiments and laboratory.*

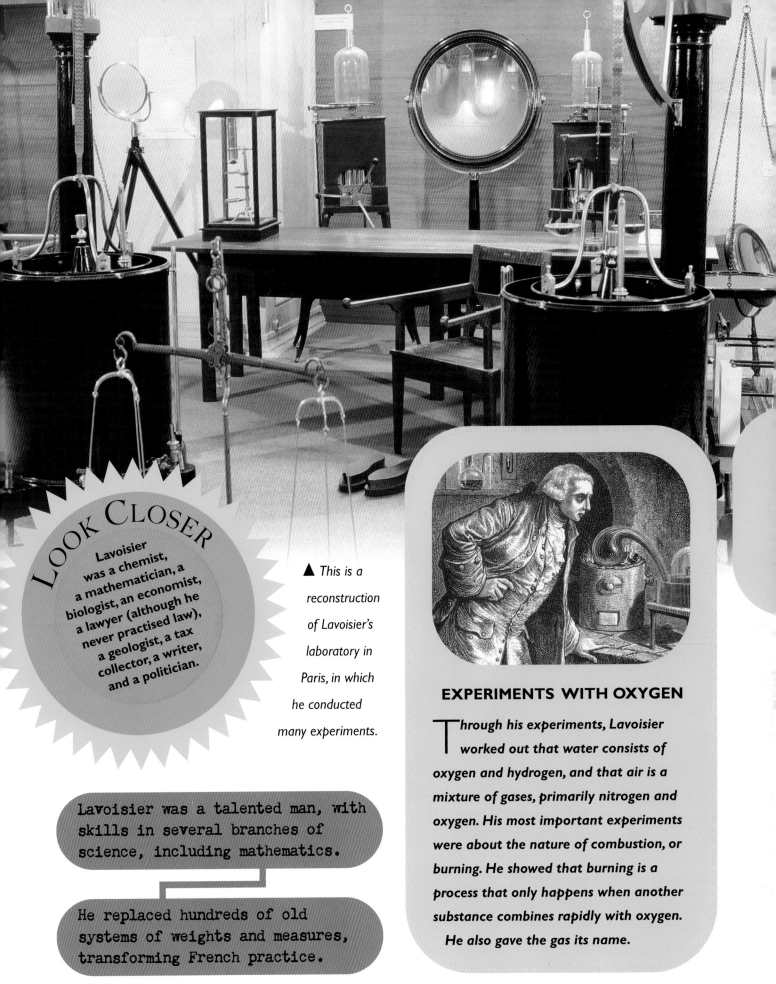

▲ This is a reconstruction of Lavoisier's laboratory in Paris, in which he conducted many experiments.

Lavoisier was a talented man, with skills in several branches of science, including mathematics.

He replaced hundreds of old systems of weights and measures, transforming French practice.

EXPERIMENTS WITH OXYGEN

Through his experiments, Lavoisier worked out that water consists of oxygen and hydrogen, and that air is a mixture of gases, primarily nitrogen and oxygen. His most important experiments were about the nature of combustion, or burning. He showed that burning is a process that only happens when another substance combines rapidly with oxygen. He also gave the gas its name.

EDWARD JENNER

A YOUNG DOCTOR WORKING IN A SMALL ENGLISH VILLAGE, JENNER SAVED COUNTLESS PEOPLE FROM SMALLPOX, A TERRIBLE DISEASE THAT KILLED 20 PERCENT OF ITS VICTIMS AND LEFT MANY OTHERS BLIND, DEAF OR HORRIBLY SCARRED.

In Jenner's day, about 10 percent of all deaths were due to smallpox. Jenner heard that people who had been ill with a disease called cowpox never caught smallpox, and decided to investigate. He infected several people with cowpox and then with a weak form of smallpox. None of them became ill, and the treatment (called vaccination after *vacca*, the Latin word for cow) was soon adopted worldwide.

LOOK CLOSER

In his spare time, Jenner studied plants and animals. It was he who discovered that, after a cuckoo lays an egg in another bird's nest, the baby cuckoo destroys the other bird's eggs.

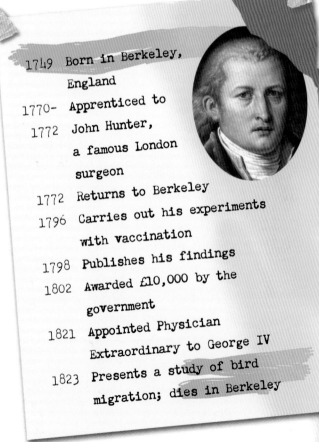

1749 Born in Berkeley, England

1770–1772 Apprenticed to John Hunter, a famous London surgeon

1772 Returns to Berkeley

1796 Carries out his experiments with vaccination

1798 Publishes his findings

1802 Awarded £10,000 by the government

1821 Appointed Physician Extraordinary to George IV

1823 Presents a study of bird migration; dies in Berkeley

A FIGURE OF FUN

When people heard about Jenner's treatment for smallpox, some of them made fun of him, like the artist who drew this cartoon showing cows sprouting from someone who Jenner has vaccinated. However, people soon began to take the smallpox vaccinations very seriously. In fact, vaccinations were made compulsory in Britain in 1853. By 1980, the disease had been wiped out throughout the world.

▼ Jenner first vaccinated 14-year-old James Phipps. He took pus from the sores of a milkmaid with cowpox (seen below). Using a thorn, he pricked James' skin and inserted the pus. James' body 'learned' to fight not only cowpox but also smallpox.

Jenner's success made him a hero and he became famous right around the world.

Jenner wrote to Napoleon in wartime requesting safe travel for two British scientists.

Napoleon agreed immediately, saying, 'We can refuse nothing to this man.'

▼ Jenner's drawing of the hand of a cowpox sufferer shows the 'pustules' from which he took the liquid that he used in his vaccinations. Milkmaids used to catch cowpox from the udders of infected cows.

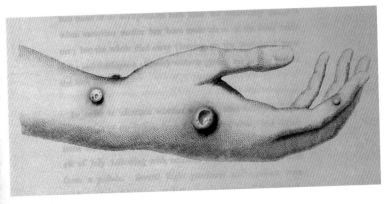

In the 19th century, the new railway networks were a visible example of the triumph of science — the trains, tracks and stations were all based on scientific discoveries and inventions.

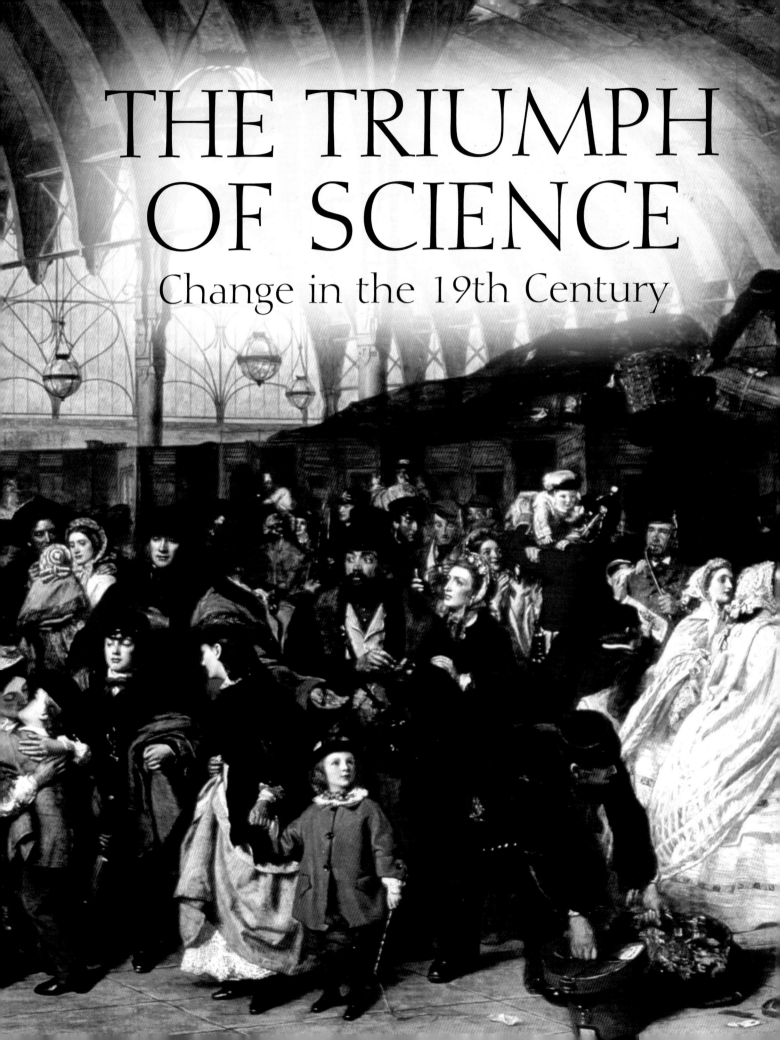

THE TRIUMPH OF SCIENCE

Change in the 19th Century

IN THE 19TH CENTURY, SCIENCE BECAME A FORCE THAT CHANGED SOCIETY COMPLETELY. IT DEVELOPED FROM A SUBJECT THAT EXPLAINED THE WORLD TO ONE THAT TRANSFORMED IT.

SCIENCE IN ACTION

SCIENTIFIC THEORIES LED TO EXCITING NEW INVENTIONS THAT INCLUDED RAILWAYS, RADIO, ELECTRICAL POWER SYSTEMS AND THE FIRST COMPUTERS.

Scientists probed even deeper into the world, and began to unlock the secrets of the atom and to understand what makes living things the way they are. Meanwhile, new conflicts arose between religion and science. Previously, most people had accepted that religious teachings were not the only way to explain things. They thought science had its place too, as long as its discoveries did not clash with beliefs. But now, thanks to Darwin, there certainly was a clash.

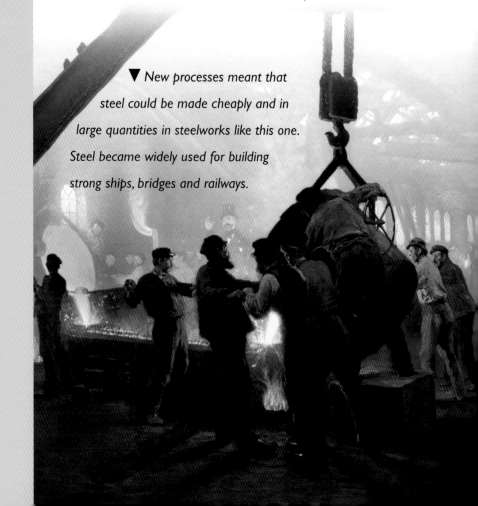

▼ New processes meant that steel could be made cheaply and in large quantities in steelworks like this one. Steel became widely used for building strong ships, bridges and railways.

CLASH OF IDEAS

In 1860, a furious debate took place in Oxford. Thomas Huxley (below right) argued that Darwin's scientific approach was the way to discover the origin of the human species. Bishop William Wilberforce (below left) disagreed. Huxley's nickname was 'Darwin's Bulldog', because of his determined defence, and Wilberforce was known as 'Soapy Sam', because of his habit of rubbing his hands together while he spoke.

▲ Many more people became interested in science, partly because of its growing importance and partly because of the work of people like Michael Faraday, who gave entertaining science lectures at the Royal Institution in London.

LOOK CLOSER

Science is not always a steady process of development. At the very end of the 19th century, discoveries about the atom showed that some of the earlier theories were wrong.

MICHAEL FARADAY

FARADAY WAS BORN IN A LONDON SLUM AND WENT ON TO BECOME ONE OF THE MOST IMPORTANT SCIENTISTS OF THE AGE THROUGH HIS DISCOVERIES IN PHYSICS AND CHEMISTRY.

His interest began with a free ticket to some science lectures, given to him by Sir Humphry Davy. Davy was a leading chemist who later employed Faraday and took him on a scientific tour of Europe.

As well as his many practical breakthroughs, Faraday also investigated the basic laws of nature, despite the lack of equipment. In his search for the laws of electricity he judged the strength of the shocks from electric eels by touching them – with his tongue!

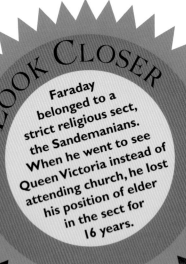

LOOK CLOSER

Faraday belonged to a strict religious sect, the Sandemanians. When he went to see Queen Victoria instead of attending church, he lost his position of elder in the sect for 16 years.

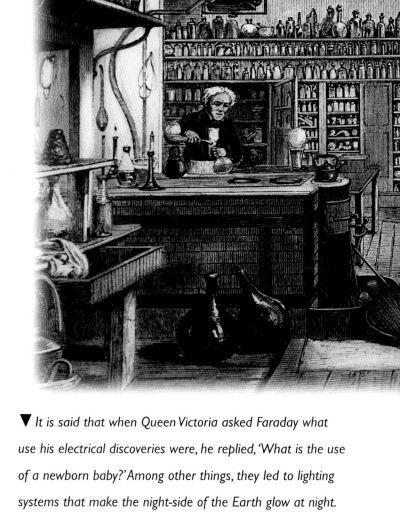

▼ It is said that when Queen Victoria asked Faraday what use his electrical discoveries were, he replied, 'What is the use of a newborn baby?' Among other things, they led to lighting systems that make the night-side of the Earth glow at night.

Faraday was the last great physicist to work without advanced mathematics.

He gave detailed explanations of his theories, defining many new technical words.

◄ Faraday's discoveries in chemistry include benzene, new types of glass and steel, and ways of turning gases into liquids.

1791 Born in London, England

1805 Apprenticed to a bookbinder

1813 Becomes Humphry Davy's chemical assistant

1821 Becomes Superintendent of the Royal Institution

1830 Becomes Professor of Chemistry

1831 Discovers the principle behind the electric motor, dynamo and transformer

1844 Is elected to the French Academy of Sciences

1867 Dies in Hampton Court, London

THE STINKING RIVER

Faraday became very famous, and was consulted on all sorts of things, from lighthouses to pollution. He wrote to The Times newspaper in 1855 about the polluted state of the River Thames, explaining that the water was so dirty that pieces of white card dropped into it rapidly vanished. This cartoon shows him giving a card to Old Father Thames.

CHARLES BABBAGE

BABBAGE DREAMED OF A WORLD WHERE MACHINES WOULD RELIEVE PEOPLE FROM BORING TASKS, SUCH AS CALCULATING TABLES OF INFORMATION, AND CARRY THOSE TASKS OUT WITHOUT MAKING MISTAKES.

Babbage was a mathematician, mechanical engineer and inventor. Thanks to his work in designing the machines that would later be called computers, his dream eventually came true. But Babbage did not live to see this. Only imperfect versions of the complicated mechanical 'engines' that he designed were built during his lifetime. Today's computers are built, not of tiny gears and wheels like Babbage's, but from electronic components that were invented long after he died.

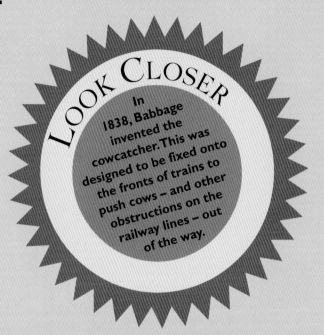

LOOK CLOSER

In 1838, Babbage invented the cowcatcher. This was designed to be fixed onto the fronts of trains to push cows – and other obstructions on the railway lines – out of the way.

1791	Born in London, England
1810–	Attends
1814	Cambridge University
1816	Elected as Fellow of the Royal Society
1819–	Builds a calculating machine
1822	he calls a Difference Engine
1823	Receives a gold medal from the Royal Astronomical Society for his Difference Engine
1836	Completes his plans for the Analytical Engine
1871	Dies in London

DIFFERENCE ENGINE

In 1991, in London's Science Museum, one of Babbage's masterpieces was finally completed. Called the Difference Engine Number 2, it weighs 2.6 tonnes and contains more than 4,000 parts. The Analytical Engine would have been far more complex. His designs for it include the basic functions of today's computers, including a memory and the ability to carry out different types of job according to its program. It would have been driven by a steam engine.

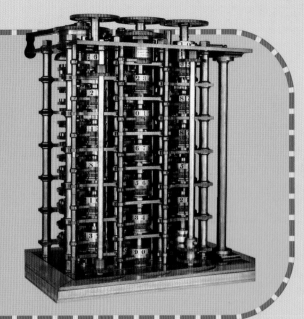

▼ In Babbage's time, fabrics with complicated patterns could be woven by machines called Jacquard looms. The patterns they made were controlled by cards with holes punched in them, and the cards could be swapped to change the pattern.

Babbage worked hard to reduce what today would be called noise pollution.

His efforts led to a law that restricted the activities of street musicians.

▲ These are the cards used to control the patterns of a Jacquard loom. Babbage planned to use very similar cards to program his engines, and early computers really did use cards in this way.

CHARLES DARWIN

ONE OF THE MOST INFLUENTIAL OF ALL SCIENTISTS, DARWIN JUST WANTED A QUIET LIFE. HOWEVER, ON A SCIENTIFIC VOYAGE, HE FOUND EVIDENCE THAT CONTRADICTED THE BELIEFS THAT MOST PEOPLE HAD ABOUT LIVING THINGS AT THAT TIME.

Darwin realized that each type of animal and plant had changed over time – an idea that caused furious debate. In every group of a single type of living things, there are many small differences. In a group of butterflies, for example, one may have darker wings than the rest. This may result in it blending in better with the trees that the butterflies rest on, so it is less likely to be eaten. That butterfly will survive and breed to produce dark-winged children. After several years, all butterflies in the area will be dark.

1809	Born in Shrewsbury, England
1825	Studies medicine at Edinburgh University
1828–1831	Studies for Bachelor of Arts degree at Cambridge University
1831–1836	Undertakes a scientific voyage on HMS *Beagle*
1859	Publishes his theory in *On the Origin of Species by Means of Natural Selection*
1871	Publishes *The Descent of Man*, developing his theory further
1882	Dies in Downe, England

▼ *During his voyage on HMS* Beagle, *Darwin visited the Galápagos Islands (below). He was interested in geology and developed a theory to explain how atolls like this one form.*

LOOK CLOSER

Darwin did not only overturn ideas about living things. His conclusion that the Earth must be very much older than the Bible implied also causes great controversy.

Darwin did not always get on well with the *Beagle*'s captain, Robert FitzRoy.

One reason for this was that FitzRoy did not like the shape of Darwin's nose!

DARWIN'S FINCHES

Key to Darwin's theory was the idea that living things evolved to fit the place where they lived. When he visited the Galápagos Islands, Darwin heard that different islands had differently shaped tortoises. He also collected many finches (above) and found that they too were different on different islands. Each island had finches whose beaks were just the right shape to eat the food, such as worms, small seeds or strong nuts, that was available on that particular island. Over many generations, the finches had evolved to suit their environments perfectly.

▲ On his voyage, Darwin experienced an earthquake, volcanic eruptions, a revolution and an attack of blood-sucking insects. He also found giant bats, huge reptiles and butterflies that clicked.

Given enough generations, tiny changes can build up to produce creatures that are very different to their ancestors – which is how, over millions of years, some dinosaurs evolved into birds.

But the Church taught that God had created people and all other living things just as they are today. So, when Darwin published his ideas, along with masses of data to prove them, angry arguments began. They continue today, though hardly any scientists doubt that Darwin's theory is correct.

▲ Darwin's study, where he wrote his many books. Nearby, Darwin had a greenhouse that was full of flesh-eating plants.

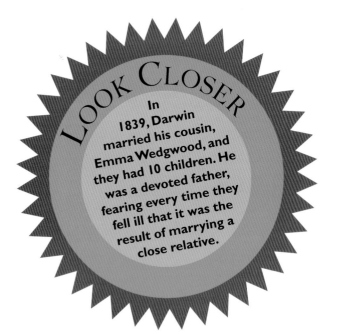

LOOK CLOSER

In 1839, Darwin married his cousin, Emma Wedgwood, and they had 10 children. He was a devoted father, fearing every time they fell ill that it was the result of marrying a close relative.

WALLACE AND DARWIN

Darwin knew his theory would upset many people, including his wife, who was a devout Christian. So he did not publish it for more than 20 years. He eventually did so because the British naturalist and explorer Alfred Russel Wallace (left, 1823–1913) came up with the same idea and wrote to him about it! The two scientists published short papers together in 1858, but the papers generated little interest at the time.

▲ *Darwin did not believe that our ancestors were monkeys, but people mocked the idea in good-humoured caricatures that appeared in the newspapers.*

SURVIVAL OF THE FITTEST

On his travels, Darwin found the remains of many animals that had become extinct. He realized that this was because other creatures, better able to survive, had taken their places. For example, the dinosaurs (above) died out when their world cooled down. The early ancestors of mammals coped with the cold better, and so were able to survive.

Darwin became ill after his voyage and never really recovered his health.

No-one knows what the illness was. It is possible that it was psychological.

GREGOR MENDEL

MENDEL WANTED TO TRANSFORM BIOLOGY IN THE WAY NEWTON HAD TRANSFORMED PHYSICS — AND HE SUCCEEDED. YET WHEN MENDEL DIED, HIS WORK WAS ALMOST UNKNOWN.

Mendel investigated why living things are similar to their parents. He found the laws that describe how the similarities are passed on from parent to child. To do this, he experimented with pea plants and with bees. He even accidentally bred a new type of bee that was so fierce the bees had to be destroyed! It was not until years after Mendel died that the importance of his published work was realized by other scientists and he became recognized as the father of genetics.

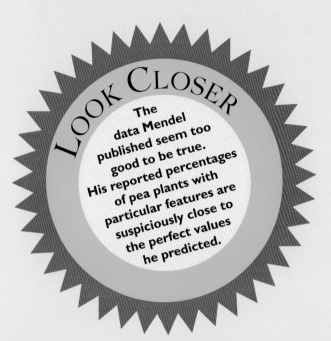

LOOK CLOSER

The data Mendel published seem too good to be true. His reported percentages of pea plants with particular features are suspiciously close to the perfect values he predicted.

▼ *Mendel was a monk for most of his life. This is the monastery garden where he bred more than 20,000 pea plants for his research. It was wrecked by a tornado in 1870 – which, as a meteorologist, Mendel quite enjoyed.*

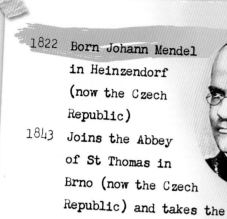

1822 Born Johann Mendel in Heinzendorf (now the Czech Republic)

1843 Joins the Abbey of St Thomas in Brno (now the Czech Republic) and takes the name Gregor

1856 Begins his study of inheritance in pea plants

1866 Publishes *Experiments in Plant Hybridization*

1868 Becomes abbot

1884 Dies in Brno

1900 Mendel's work is rediscovered

In 1865, Mendel gave two presentations to explain his work on inheritance.

It is said that no one asked a single question at either of these presentations.

▼ This is a 19th-century teaching tool, containing plant specimens, from the Mendel Museum. Very few of Mendel's original research materials survive because his successor as abbot, Anselm Rambousek, destroyed most of them.

THE LAWS OF INHERITANCE

Mendel realized that there are structures now called alleles in our bodies that control many characteristics – such as eye colour – and that they exist in pairs. When two people have children, each child inherits one eye-colour allele from each parent. Only children who inherit two blue-eye alleles will have blue eyes. If they have one brown and one blue allele, their eyes will be brown. Because the brown-eye allele 'takes control' of the eye colour in this way, it is called 'dominant'. The blue-eye allele is called 'recessive'. Now, we know that all the biological information that is passed on by parents to their children is contained in structures called genes.

LOUIS PASTEUR

L OUIS PASTEUR SET HIMSELF HIGH STANDARDS. WHEN HE SAT AN EXAM FOR THE BEST SCHOOL IN PARIS, HE CAME FIFTEENTH. THIS WAS GOOD ENOUGH TO GET IN, BUT HE STUDIED ANOTHER YEAR AND RETOOK THE EXAM, COMING FOURTH.

His standards were just as high when it came to science. Through his hard work, he saved more lives than any other scientist. He developed vaccinations for anthrax, rabies and other diseases, and proved how germs spread. He also invented a heat treatment, called pasteurization, to kill germs in wine. Today, this is used all over the world to make milk safe to drink.

Towards the end of his life, the Pasteur Institute opened in Paris, with Louis as its first director. It has continued his fight against diseases ever since.

▶ *Pasteur, played by the French actor Bernard Fresson, is shown working in his laboratory in the television film,* Pasteur. *The scientist became world-famous and was called in to deal with a plague that was wiping out silkworms in many countries.*

1822	Born in Dole, France
1849	Becomes Professor of Chemistry at Strasbourg University
1854	Becomes Professor of Chemistry at Lille University
1865	Patents pasteurization
1881	Develops a vaccine against anthrax for sheep
1885	Successfully tests rabies vaccine on a boy bitten by a rabid dog
1888	Pasteur Institute opens
1895	Dies in Paris, France

LOOK CLOSER

Pasteur helped develop the theory that each disease is caused by a particular sort of germ. He became obsessed by germs, often refusing to shake hands with his friends to avoid infection.

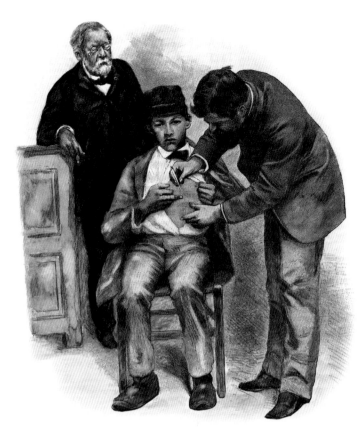

At the time, it was thought germs formed 'spontaneously', from dead matter.

Pasteur's experiments showed that germs are in fact produced by other germs.

◀ *Pasteur tested his vaccine on a boy bitten by a rabid dog, at great risk to the boy — luckily, it worked! The vaccine can give protection even after someone is bitten.*

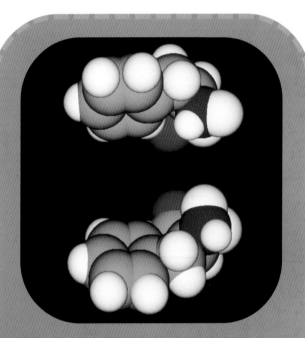

MIRROR IMAGES

Pasteur's early scientific work was as a chemist. He discovered chemicals that had identical ingredients, but that exist in pairs of mirror-like structures (represented in the artwork above). These structures change the way that the chemicals they are part of affect living things. For example, one these structures treats tuberculosis, but its mirror-image version causes blindness.

JAMES CLERK MAXWELL

JAMES CLERK MAXWELL WAS CALLED 'DAFTY' AT SCHOOL, BUT WHEN HE WAS ONLY 15 YEARS OLD, HE INVENTED A MECHANICAL WAY OF DRAWING CURVED SHAPES WITH A PIECE OF TWINE THAT WAS PUBLISHED BY EDINBURGH'S ROYAL SOCIETY.

Maxwell became one of the most important of all physicists, making discoveries in biology, electricity and magnetism, astronomy and thermodynamics (the science of heat). In 1874, he set up the Cavendish Laboratory, one of the most advanced laboratories in the world. Sadly, he was not in charge of it for long – he died in 1879, aged only 48. In his short life, he published many scientific papers about his discoveries and he wrote poems about science as well.

MAXWELL'S DEMON

Maxwell helped to develop the kinetic theory of gases, which explains that heat is the motion of molecules. Heat spreads from a warmer area to a cooler one. Maxwell imagined a demon opening and closing a tiny door to let fast molecules (red) collect in one area and slow ones (blue) in another. This would reverse the process and make heat flow from a cooler area to a warmer one. Later scientists proved that even a demon could not do this.

1831 Born in Edinburgh, Scotland

1860–1865 Professor at King's College, London

1861 Elected to the Royal Society of London

1864 Publishes key equations relating electricity and magnetism

1871 Becomes first Professor of Cavendish Laboratory, Cambridge

1879 Dies of a heart attack in Cambridge, England

1887 Radio waves Maxwell predicted are discovered by Heinrich Hertz.

Maxwell discovered and published the laws that link electricity and magnetism.

His laws - Maxwell's equations - revealed that light is an electromagnetic wave.

Maxwell also used the laws to predict the existence of radio waves.

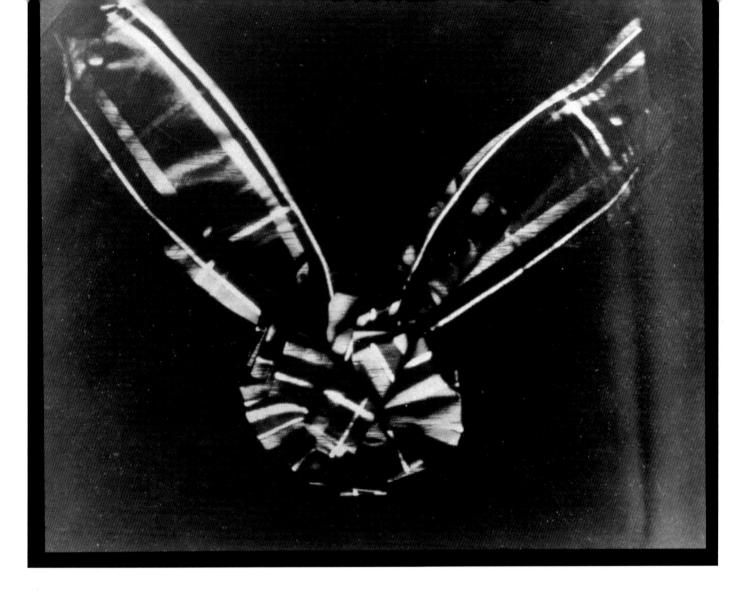

▲ *In 1861, Maxwell made this colour photograph — the first in the world — of a tartan ribbon. He took three photographs, each with a different colour filter, and put them together.*

LOOK CLOSER

Maxwell proved that the rings of Saturn must be made of many tiny solid objects, because if they were solid rings, or were made of liquid or gas, they would fall apart.

THE DOGSTOPPER

Maxwell had a pet terrier with which he loved to perform different tricks. In particular, the dog was fond of running round in a circle chasing his tail. Maxwell's friends would sometimes encourage the dog to do this, but, although it was easy to get the dog started, only Maxwell could stop him. He did this by moving his hand in a circle first one way, then the other. Each time his hand changed direction, the dog would too. Gradually, Maxwell moved his hand less and less, and the dog would slow down too, and finally stop.

DMITRI MENDELEYEV

EVERYTHING IN THE UNIVERSE IS MADE FROM AROUND 100 'ELEMENTS'. ON EARTH, MOST ELEMENTS ARE COMBINED WITH OTHER ELEMENTS, AND SEPARATING THEM CAN BE TRICKY. HOWEVER, SEPARATING THEM IS NOT AS HARD AS PREDICTING THE EXISTENCE OF NEW ONES.

Russian chemist Dmitri Mendeleyev set out to list all the known elements by their weights. He discovered the pattern of the elements, a pattern with gaps that he correctly predicted must one day be filled. It is his attempt to classify the elements according to their chemical properties that formed the basis for the modern periodic table. It is said that he literally dreamed up the idea!

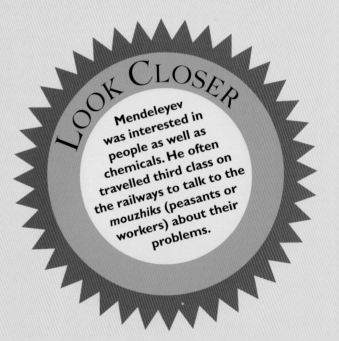

KEY TO TABLE

- Non metals
- Alkali metals
- Alkaline metals
- Transition metals

▲ This is a modern periodic table containing all the elements now known. The columns are called groups and the rows are periods.

NOBLE GASES

The elements in the final column of the periodic table hardly react at all with other elements, and are called noble gases. The seven noble gases that occur are helium, neon, argon, krypton, xenon, radon and ununoctium. Here, the element neon is made to glow brightly by passing electricity through it.

LOOK CLOSER

Mendeleyev was interested in people as well as chemicals. He often travelled third class on the railways to talk to the mouzhiks (peasants or workers) about their problems.

■ Noble gases
■ Metalloids
■ Halogens
□ Other metals
■ Rare earth elements

							2 **He** Helium
	5 **B** Boron	6 **C** Carbon	7 **N** Nitrogen	8 **O** Oxygen	9 **F** Fluorine	10 **Ne** Neon	
	13 **Al** Aluminium	14 **Si** Silicon	15 **P** Phosphorus	16 **S** Sulphur	17 **Cl** Chlorine	18 **Ar** Argon	

27 **Co** Cobalt	28 **Ni** Nickel	29 **Cu** Copper	30 **Zn** Zinc	31 **Ga** Gallium	32 **Ge** Germanium	33 **As** Arsenic	34 **Se** Selenium	35 **Br** Bromine	36 **Kr** Krypton
45 **Rh** Rhodium	46 **Pd** Palladium	47 **Ag** Silver	48 **Cd** Cadmium	49 **In** Indium	50 **Sn** Tin	51 **Sb** Antimony	52 **Te** Tellurium	53 **I** Iodine	54 **Xe** Xenon
77 **Ir** Iridium	78 **Pt** Platinum	79 **Au** Gold	80 **Hg** Mercury	81 **Tl** Thallium	82 **Pb** Lead	83 **Bi** Bismuth	84 **Po** Polonium	85 **At** Astatine	86 **Rn** Radon
109 **Mt** Meitnerium	110 **Uun** Ununnilium	111 **Uuu** Unununium	112 **Uub** Ununbium	113 **Uut** Ununtrium	114 **Uuq** Ununquadium	115 **Uup** Ununpentium	116 **Uuh** Ununhexium	117 **Uus** Ununseptium	118 **Uuo** Ununoctium

64 **Gd** Gadolinium	65 **Tb** Terbium	66 **Dy** Dysprosium	67 **Ho** Holmium	68 **Er** Erbium	69 **Tm** Thulium	70 **Yb** Ytterbium	71 **Lu** Lutetium
96 **Cm** Curium	97 **Bk** Berkelium	98 **Cf** Californium	99 **Es** Einsteinium	100 **Fm** Fermium	101 **Md** Mendelevium	102 **No** Nobelium	103 **Lr** Lawrencium

▼ *Mendeleyev arranged the elements he knew in this table, in order of the increasing weight of the atoms. Each column contains elements with similar properties.*

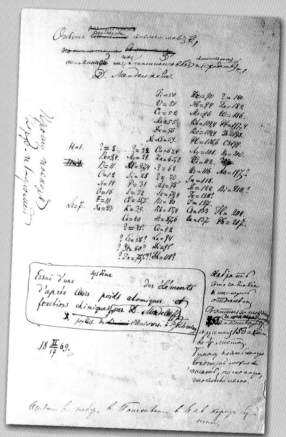

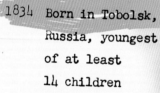

1834 Born in Tobolsk, Russia, youngest of at least 14 children

1856 Graduates from university in St Petersburg

1866 Becomes Professor of Chemistry at St Petersburg University

1869 Constructs his periodic table

1891 Resigns professorship to support a student protest

1893 Appointed Director of the Bureau of Weights and Measures

1909 Dies of flu in St Petersburg

1955 Element 101 is named Mendelevium

Mendeleyev was famous for his scruffiness, particularly as he grew older.

He only cut his hair and beard once a year, despite a request from Tsar Alexander III.

One observer said about his appearance, 'Every hair acted separate from the others.'

WILHELM RÖNTGEN

O N AN AUTUMN EVENING IN 1895, WILHELM RÖNTGEN WAS STUDYING THE EFFECTS OF ELECTRICITY ON GASES. SUDDENLY, ACROSS HIS DARKENED LABORATORY IN THE UNIVERSITY OF WÜRZBURG, HE WAS SURPRISED TO SEE A GHOSTLY GLOW.

The glow came from some chemical-coated paper. He realized the chemicals must be responding to unknown rays from his equipment. Röntgen called them X-rays. He found that these rays pass through flesh but not so easily through bone – as a startling glimpse of his own living skeleton demonstrated. Scientists now know that X-rays, light and radio-waves all belong to the electromagnetic spectrum.

In 1901, Röntgen was awarded the first-ever Nobel Prize for Physics.

He donated all the prize money to his university, the University of Munich.

▼ *Röntgen discovered how to take photographs using X-rays, including this one, the first ever, of his wife's hand. It is said that she gasped, 'I have seen my death!'*

1845 Born in Lennep (in what is now Germany)

1879 Becomes Professor of Physics at Giessen

1888 Becomes Professor of Physics at Würzburg, Germany

1895 Discovers X-rays and publishes paper *On a New Kind of Rays*

1900 Becomes Professor of Physics at Munich

1901 Receives the Nobel Prize for Physics

1923 Dies in Munich, Germany

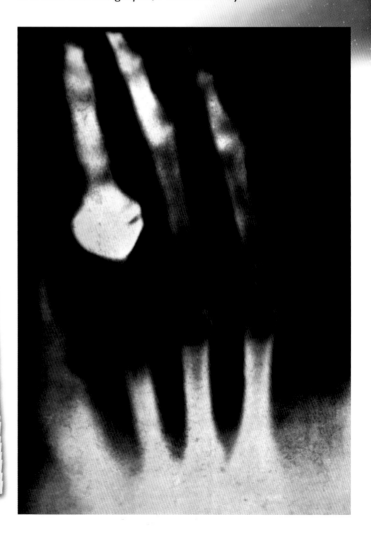

▲ X-rays are not only made in laboratories, they are also produced in nature. One very powerful natural source was discovered in 1964, about 60 trillion kilometres from Earth in the constellation of Cygnus (above). X-rays are generated by the destruction of matter as it falls into a black hole.

LOOK CLOSER

Röntgen was expelled from his school when he was wrongly accused of drawing a cartoon of one of his teachers. Although he knew who had drawn it, he refused to say who it was.

THE NOVELTY OF X-RAYS

X-rays generated a lot of interest and excitement. This was partly because doctors could now look inside the bodies of patients without needing to cut them open. However, it was also partly because of the weird images they produced – and many cartoons like this one appeared.

MARIE CURIE

MARIE CURIE DEVOTED HERSELF TO SCIENCE – BUT IT COST HER HER LIFE. TOGETHER WITH HER HUSBAND AND FELLOW SCIENTIST PIERRE CURIE, SHE DISCOVERED TWO NEW ELEMENTS, POLONIUM AND RADIUM.

Extracting these two elements required hard physical labour from Marie as well as great scientific skill. She had to process more than a tonne of pitchblende ore to obtain only 0.1g of radium. At the time, radium was an element unlike any other – it never becomes cool, it turns from white to black in moments and it glows in the dark. Radium is a radioactive element, which means that it produces radiation. It was soon being used to treat some forms of cancer and people thought it was almost magical. But it was also deadly. Marie Curie's death was caused by exposure to radiation, and to this day her notebooks are dangerously radioactive.

A SCIENTIFIC ROMANCE

One of Pierre's first gifts to Marie was a paper he had written about crystallography. And when Marie was asked what wedding dress she would like, she asked for a dark one so she could re-use it for working in her laboratory. She and Pierre loved the countryside and went on many cycling trips together. In this picture, Marie's clothes are unusually fashionable. She had little interest in clothes and only bought herself a new hat for a scientific visit to the United States.

LOOK CLOSER

During World War I, Marie developed a fleet of 18 X-ray cars, which meant wounded soldiers could be examined without the dangers of moving them. She sometimes drove cars herself.

1867 Born Maria Sklodowska, in Warsaw, Poland
1891 Moves to Paris to study
1895 Marries Pierre
1898 The Curies discover polonium and radium
1903 The Curies and Henri Becquerel jointly awarded Nobel Prize for Physics – Marie was the first woman to be awarded a Nobel Prize
1906 Pierre killed in road accident
1911 Marie awarded second Nobel Prize, this time for Chemistry
1921 Tours USA to raise research funds
1929 Second tour of USA
1934 Dies of cancer in Passy, France

◀ After Pierre died in a road accident, Marie continued their work alone. Marie's sister Bronislawa was also a scientist, and Marie's daughter and son-in-law were jointly awarded a Nobel Prize for Chemistry.

In Marie's time, there were very few universities that accepted female students.

With little money, and only a few words of French, Marie went to the Sorbonne in Paris.

There, she obtained degrees in both Physics and the Mathematical Sciences.

RADIOACTIVITY

Radium produces radiation because its atoms are unstable – they break down suddenly and release fast-moving particles and a great deal of energy. Some of this energy in radium is the light and heat that Marie noticed. Radioactive elements are both useful and dangerous. They can be used to make nuclear power stations, cancer treatments and smoke detectors, but they can also cause cancer and birth defects, and nuclear weapons are made from them. Since Marie Curie discovered radium, more than 30 other radioactive elements have been isolated.

ERNEST RUTHERFORD

ERNEST RUTHERFORD, A FARMER'S SON FROM NEW ZEALAND, BECAME A BARON, A PROFESSOR AT TWO UNIVERSITIES, PRESIDENT OF THE ROYAL SOCIETY AND THE INSTITUTE OF PHYSICS, AND DIRECTOR OF THE CAVENDISH LABORATORY IN CAMBRIDGE, AS WELL AS WINNING A NOBEL PRIZE IN 1908.

He could be a somewhat scary and demanding scientist. He used to sing loudly in his laboratory and earned the nickname 'the crocodile'. He occasionally got tripped up by his own maths during lectures and would then call his audience 'numbskulls' for not correcting him. But he was one of the greatest ever experimental physicists. He was also one of science's great leaders, building teams of dedicated followers.

▶ *This looks nothing like a modern laboratory, but in this laboratory at Cambridge University, and others like it, Rutherford and his colleagues developed the new science of nuclear physics.*

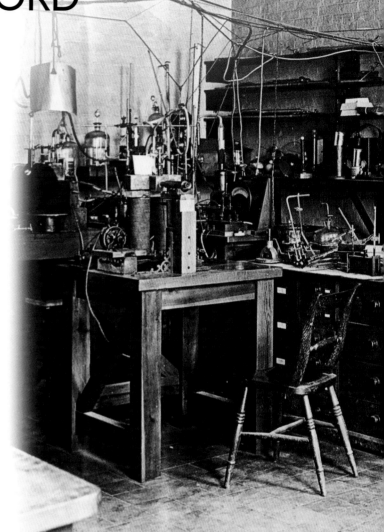

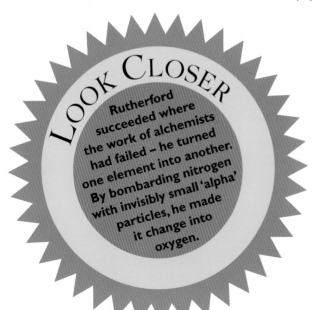

LOOK CLOSER

Rutherford succeeded where the work of alchemists had failed – he turned one element into another. By bombarding nitrogen with invisibly small 'alpha' particles, he made it change into oxygen.

Rutherford suggested that radioactivity could be used to date rock samples.

Today, it is now the main method that scientists use to date ancient objects.

Rutherford's method showed that the Earth is 4,540 million years old.

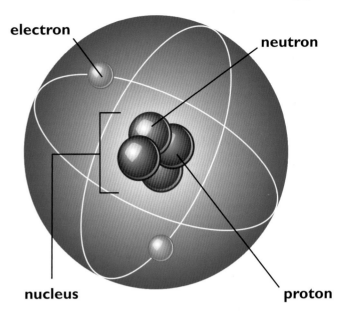

electron — neutron — nucleus — proton

▲ *Rutherford's experiments showed that atoms are almost all empty space, with a tiny dense nucleus at the centre. In this diagram of a helium atom the nucleus has been enlarged. It is really only about 0.001% the width of the whole atom.*

1871 Born in Spring Grove, New Zealand, one of 12 children
1895 Moves to England to work at Cambridge University
1898 Discovers the alpha and beta particles that form part of nuclear radiation
1910 Discovers the atomic nucleus
1919 Causes the first nuclear reaction, in which one element is changed into another
1931 Created Baron Rutherford
1937 Dies in Cambridge, England

RUTHERFORD AND GEIGER

Rutherford helped his students become great scientists. The scientist on the left is Hans Geiger, famous for developing the Geiger counter, which is used to detect radioactivity. The two men also worked together to study the structure of atoms by firing tiny particles at atoms of gold.

A boy is transfixed while playing a computer game in a special booth, his surroundings enhanced by laser beams and special effects.

REVOLUTIONS IN SCIENCE

New Discoveries
Transform the World

IN THE EARLY

20TH CENTURY,

NEW DISCOVERIES

TRANSFORMED

SCIENCE. MORE

SCIENTISTS WERE

BEING TRAINED

THAN EVER BEFORE

AND SCIENCE BEGAN

TO HAVE MORE

INFLUENCE

ON SOCIETY.

REVELATIONS!

IN THE FIRST DECADES OF THE 20TH CENTURY, THERE WAS A REVOLUTION IN SCIENCE – NEW DISCOVERIES ABOUT THE LARGEST AND THE SMALLEST OBJECTS IN THE UNIVERSE SHOWED THAT THEY OBEYED DIFFERENT SCIENTIFIC LAWS TO THOSE THAT CONTROLLED MORE FAMILIAR THINGS.

Scientists discovered that the Universe is expanding, and that space and time can behave in strange and unexpected ways. Various areas of science underwent major changes. These included medicine, where new treatments and preventive measures saved millions of lives.

Technology also advanced rapidly, with the invention of the first aeroplanes, the mass-production of cars and the introduction of the first regular radio broadcasts.

▲ As travel and communication became easier, scientists met at conferences. This one in Brussels in 1911 included Rutherford, Curie and Einstein, along with other great scientists of the time.

▲ *Einstein's insight into space and time has led to the possibility that, one day, we may be able to use the 'warp drive' that is so popular in science fiction to travel to the stars.*

LOOK CLOSER

In 1901, the first annual Nobel Prizes were awarded, in Sweden, to those who had made the greatest contributions to Physics, Chemistry, Medicine, Literature and Peace.

NUCLEAR PHYSICS

One of the key breakthroughs of the 20th century was nuclear physics. At the beginning of the century, some scientists did not even believe in the existence of atoms. By the time the world was approaching the end of the century, other scientists had worked out the structure of atoms. What is more, by using nuclear physics, they had learned to release and control the vast energies within the atoms.

World War I (1914-1918) resulted in the deaths of many young scientists.

However, the war also encouraged the very rapid development of technology.

ALBERT EINSTEIN

THE UNIVERSE APPEARS TO BE A COMPLICATED PLACE, BUT ALBERT EINSTEIN, ONE OF THE GREATEST SCIENTISTS OF ALL, BELIEVED THAT ITS SECRET IS AN UNDERLYING SIMPLICITY.

He spent his life in search of that simplicity, showing that mass, energy, space, time, gravity and motion are all just different ways of looking at the same things. Scientists today are continuing his quest for one simple 'Theory of Everything'.

Einstein's theories are mathematical – but for him, the maths was the final stage of the process. His breakthroughs began with his vivid imagination.

LOOK CLOSER

When Einstein's wife was shown round an enormous telescope and told that it was for working out the shape of the Universe, she said, 'My husband does that on an old envelope.'

▼ Einstein made many of his discoveries in 1905, while he was employed as a clerk at the Swiss Patent Office in Bern.

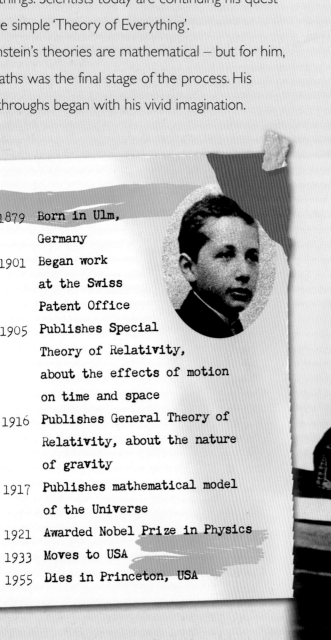

1879	Born in Ulm, Germany
1901	Began work at the Swiss Patent Office
1905	Publishes Special Theory of Relativity, about the effects of motion on time and space
1916	Publishes General Theory of Relativity, about the nature of gravity
1917	Publishes mathematical model of the Universe
1921	Awarded Nobel Prize in Physics
1933	Moves to USA
1955	Dies in Princeton, USA

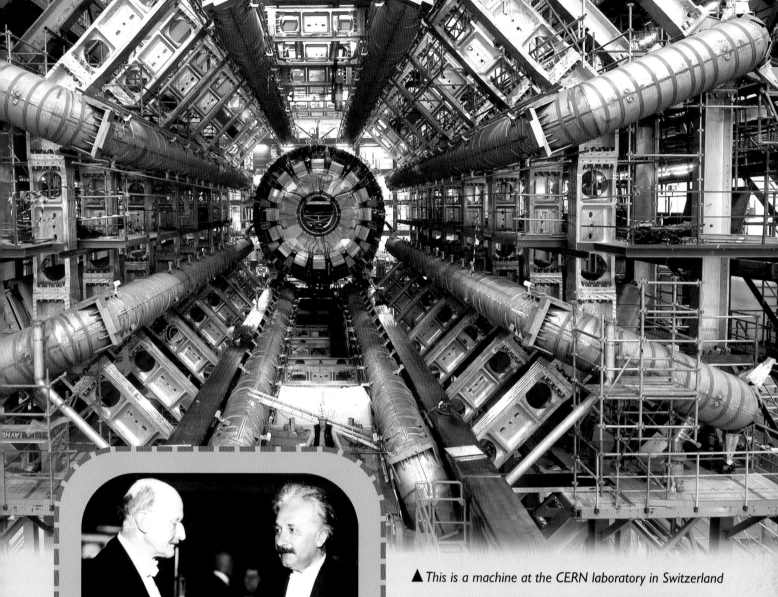

▲ This is a machine at the CERN laboratory in Switzerland that accelerates particles at enormous speed. As Einstein predicted, the particles get heavier as they speed up.

EINSTEIN AND PLANCK

Max Planck (left) published Einstein's first papers, and the men became friends and colleagues who collaborated for many years. Planck discovered that hot objects store energy in tiny batches. Einstein developed this discovery into the theory that light is made of these batches (now called photons), which sometimes behave as particles and sometimes as waves.

Einstein's discoveries suggested that it was possible to make atomic weapons.

In 1939, he wrote to the US president, Franklin Roosevelt, to tell him this.

Soon afterwards, the USA began to build an atom bomb – without telling Einstein!

Einstein puzzled over questions such as 'What would it be like to ride a light-ray?' and 'What does falling off a house feel like, and why?' The answers often turned out to be very strange indeed. Einstein found out that mass is a type of energy, showed that light is a strange cross between particles and waves, discovered what gravity really is, explained how to change the flow of time and even proved why the sky is blue!

Einstein also had a passionate interest in politics, and spent years campaigning for peaceful cooperation between countries and warning everyone of the dangers of nuclear weapons. His political work did not change the world, but his science did.

LOOK CLOSER

In 1952, Einstein was very surprised when he was asked to become president of Israel. He thought that perhaps he had better stick to science, and turned down the offer.

◄ In 1933, Einstein and his wife moved to the United States to escape the control of the Nazis, who had persecuted him by seizing his money and burning his publications. Here, he is lecturing at the Mount Wilson Observatory in California.

▼ Einstein's famous equation, E=mc², is a mathematical way of saying that mass is a form of energy. In the equation, E is energy, m is mass, and c is the speed of light (299,792,458 metres per second). So a tiny amount of mass is really a huge amount of energy.

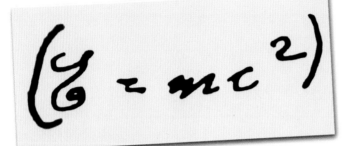

▼ Einstein showed how gravity works. Massive objects 'warp' space and time, a bit like the dent a heavy object makes in a sheet of rubber. This picture shows the Earth warping the area around it. Objects such as the satellite follow the curves in space and time when they orbit the Earth.

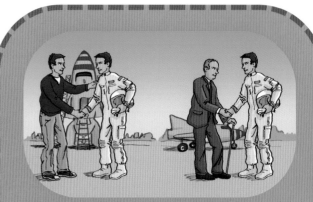

THE TWIN PARADOX

Einstein suggested that time slows down at very high speeds. If an astronaut makes a long journey in a spaceship that travels at many thousands of kilometres a second, he could return to Earth to find that he is much younger than his identical twin brother. The effect can also be seen when very accurate clocks are flown on fast planes. A clock on a plane gets very slightly out of step in its timing with clocks on the ground. Einstein found that both high-speed motion and strong gravity slow down time.

ALEXANDER FLEMING

ALEXANDER FLEMING HAD VERY SHARP EYES. IN 1928, WHEN HE RETURNED FROM A HOLIDAY TO HIS JOB AS A MEDICAL RESEARCHER, HE SPOTTED SOMETHING STRANGE IN THE LABORATORY.

Fleming had been breeding patches of germs in culture dishes, and one dish had gone mouldy. This was not unusual, but what Fleming noticed was very odd indeed. The patches of germs growing near the mould were smaller than the rest. Somehow, the mould was killing them. Years later, this lucky discovery, which led to the isolation of the antibiotic medicine penicillin, would save millions of lives.

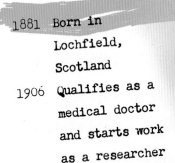

1881 Born in Lochfield, Scotland

1906 Qualifies as a medical doctor and starts work as a researcher

1914– Serves as a captain in the
1918 Army Medical Corps in World War I

1928 Discovers penicillin in mould

1929 Publishes his discovery

1940 Florey and Chain discover how to extract pure penicillin from mould

1945 Fleming, Florey and Chain awarded Nobel Prize for Medicine

1955 Dies in London, England

In 1946, Fleming suggested that some germs might evolve defences against antibiotics.

Today, 'superbugs' like this are a major problem throughout the health system.

A MODERN MIRACLE

Penicillin is an antibiotic – a substance that is harmless to people but that kills some types of germ (the word antibiotic means 'against life'). During World War II (1939–1945), many people thought that England would be invaded by Germany. They feared that valuable stocks of penicillin extracts might be seized, so researchers smeared it on the insides of their coats so that some of it would be kept safe.

◀ *Penicillin being grown in the laboratory*

◀ *Fleming, seen here at work in his laboratory, found that the mould he had discovered was harmless (which was just as well since his assistant ate some of it). But he could not find a way to extract the germ-killing substance, which he named penicillin, from the mould.*

LOOK CLOSER

A decade after Fleming discovered penicillin, two scientists, Howard Florey and Ernst Chain, extracted it from mould. They found it could be used to cure deadly infections.

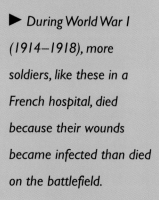

▶ *During World War I (1914–1918), more soldiers, like these in a French hospital, died because their wounds became infected than died on the battlefield.*

NIELS BOHR

NIELS BOHR LOVED TO DEVELOP REALLY WEIRD THEORIES, BUT LIKE MANY SCIENTISTS OF HIS TIME, BOHR'S WORK WAS INTERRUPTED BY THE OUTBREAK OF WORLD WAR II.

Bohr fled from his native occupied Denmark to Sweden in a fishing-boat, and then reached the safety of England in the bomb-hold of a plane. He left his Nobel Prize medal behind him – having first dissolved it in acid to stop it from being stolen. Sure enough, the liquid was left alone, and after the war the gold was extracted from it and the medal re-made.

Towards the end of the war, Bohr helped to develop the atom bomb in the USA, but he also worked hard for peace after the war. He devoted himself to the peaceful application of atomic power, trying to convince the world that nuclear weapons should be kept under international control.

1885 Born in Copenhagen, Denmark

1903 Attends University of Copenhagen

1912 Works with Rutherford in the UK

1913 Publishes theory of atomic structure

1921 Founds the Institute of Theoretical Physics in Denmark

1922 Receives Nobel Prize for Physics

1943 Escapes from Denmark and joins atom bomb project in the USA

1955 Organizes 'Atoms for Peace' conference in Geneva

1962 Dies in Copenhagen, Denmark

▲ *Bohr believed that, in the world of atoms, things are not real in the way everyday objects are. His colleague Einstein (left) disagreed. Many scientists now believe Bohr was right.*

A heated element can produce light containing a unique spectrum of colours.

This spectrum shows the element is producing light-particles with precise energies.

Bohr's theory correctly predicted the energies and colours produced by hydrogen.

◀ *Bohr joined the USA's secret Manhattan Project, which was developing the first atom bomb, though he argued that discoveries about the atom should not be kept secret.*

LOOK CLOSER

Bohr was an excellent footballer, but he might have been better still if he had not been a scientist. He once left a goal open because he was writing calculations on the goal-post!

SECRETS OF THE ATOM

Ernest Rutherford (pages 88–9) had shown that atoms have tiny, dense cores that are surrounded by fast-moving electrons. But there was still a mystery to be solved. The electrons should quickly spiral in on the nucleus, losing all their energy on the way, and atoms should simply shrivel up. In order to explain why this does not happen, Bohr suggested that the electrons can only exist at certain distances from an atomic nucleus, and that they cannot lose their energy gradually. If they lose any energy at all, it has to be in lumps (now called quanta).

EDWIN HUBBLE

EDWIN HUBBLE WAS FASCINATED BY THE STARS, AND EVEN MORE INTERESTED IN THE PATCHES OF CLOUDY LIGHT CALLED NEBULAE. WHAT HE DISCOVERED ABOUT NEBULAE IDENTIFIED EARTH'S PLACE IN THE UNIVERSE.

Hubble found that the enormous galaxy that the Sun is part of, and which contains billions of stars, is just one of many galaxies that are scattered through the Universe. Later, Hubble and his colleagues showed that the whole, vast Universe is expanding. He and Milton Humason formulated the Redshift Distance Law of Galaxies, now known as Hubble's Law. Hubble was able to measure how fast the galaxies that make up the Universe are moving away from each other. From this, other scientists worked out that the Universe is unbelievably old – it has lasted thousands of times longer than the human race.

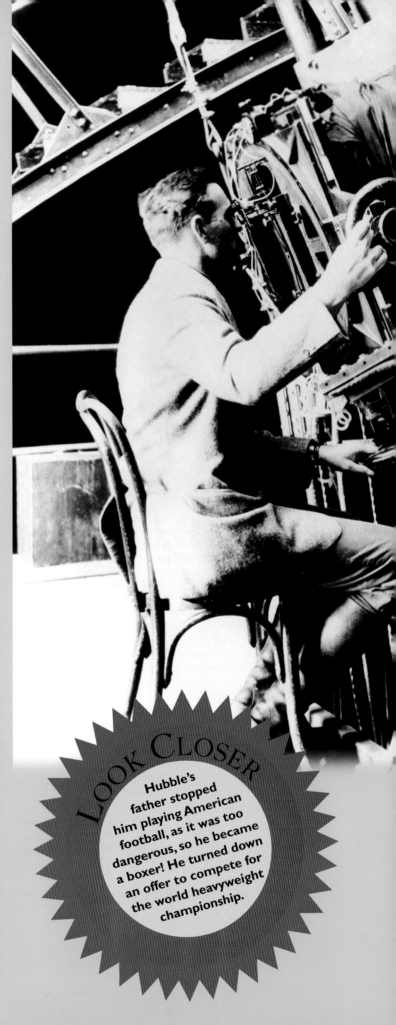

▼ *This is the Andromeda nebula. Hubble proved that it is a separate galaxy to the Milky Way Galaxy that contains Earth.*

LOOK CLOSER

Hubble's father stopped him playing American football, as it was too dangerous, so he became a boxer! He turned down an offer to compete for the world heavyweight championship.

CEPHEID VARIABLE STARS

Finding the distance to a star is not easy — unless the star is a Cepheid variable. Cepheid stars have periods of dimness (above right) followed by periods of brightness (below right). These periods occur regularly, so scientists can work out how far away a particular Cepheid star must be. Hubble found Cepheid stars in the Andromeda galaxy and used them to find out how far away the galaxy was — his answer was an amazing 10 billion billion kilometres! Today, we know it is even further.

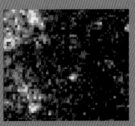

Star is large, cool and dim

Star is small, hot and bright

◀ *Hubble's excellent hand-to-eye coordination was useful both for army target practice and when he used his telescopes.*

Hubble **volunteered to fight** in World War I, and tested weapons in World War II.

But he was opposed to nuclear weapons and campaigned **vigorously against their use.**

1889 Born in Marshfield, USA

1910 Graduates in science from the University of Chicago

1919 Joins Mount Wilson Observatory, which has the world's largest telescope

1923 Proves that the Milky Way Galaxy is not the only one

1925 Suggests a way of classifying galaxies

1929 Formulates 'Hubble's Law', helping to prove that the Universe is expanding

1953 Dies in San Marino, USA

THE BIG BANG

Hubble's Law has helped to establish that the Universe began about 13.7 billion years ago in an event called the Big Bang, and that it has been expanding ever since. Scientists can still measure the glow of radiation from the Big Bang, although it has cooled down to a temperature of −270°C. Astronomers think that the Universe will eventually become completely dark, cold and dead, and will go on expanding forever.

WERNER HEISENBERG

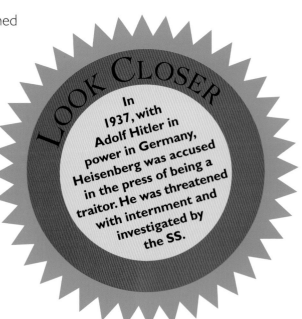

HEISENBERG WAS A PROFESSOR OF PHYSICS AT LEIPZIG UNIVERSITY WHEN WORLD WAR II BROKE OUT IN 1939. HE HELPED TO RESEARCH THE ATOM BOMB FOR THE NAZIS, BUT MAY HAVE PLANNED TO USE HIS POSITION TO HALT THE PROJECT. HOWEVER, HE WAS ARRESTED IN 1945 BECAUSE OF THE RESEARCH AND HELD IN ENGLAND.

Heisenberg's discoveries opened the door to a strange new world of physics. And weird things happen in the physics that Heisenberg helped to develop. His Uncertainty Principle states that it is impossible to know exactly where a particle is and at the same time to know how fast it is moving. This means that it is impossible to describe exactly what happens in the world. When Heisenberg said that there are limits to what we can possibly find out, this struck at the heart of physics, which had always assumed that everything could one day be discovered.

LOOK CLOSER

In 1937, with Adolf Hitler in power in Germany, Heisenberg was accused in the press of being a traitor. He was threatened with internment and investigated by the SS.

◀ *Heisenberg is pictured with his fellow Nobel Prize-winners Enrico Fermi (left) and Wolfgang Pauli (right). With other scientists, they developed nuclear physics and nuclear power.*

◀ *Superconductors are materials that have no resistance to electricity, and Heisenberg helped to explain how they work. If a magnet approaches a superconductor, it makes an electrical current flow in it. The current creates a magnetic field, which repels the magnet and makes it float. Here, a magnet is floating above a nitrogen-cooled superconducting ceramic.*

1901 Born in Würzburg, Germany

1925 Publishes his version of quantum mechanics

1927 Formulates Uncertainty Principle

1932 Awarded the Nobel Prize for Physics for his development of quantum mechanics

1939 Is one of the leading scientists investigating nuclear fission

1945 Arrested by US troops and held in England

1946 Becomes director of the Max Planck Institute in Germany

1976 Dies in Munich

TINY WAVE PATTERNS

When electrons were discovered, people thought that they were simply tiny particles. But then scientists found that they make patterns like the one above, as if they are waves. Heisenberg realized that electrons and other tiny things are so different to everyday objects that no-one can really imagine them. However, he could use mathematics to describe them exactly. His work helps us to understand how the world works at a sub-microscopic level.

Computers have become essential tools for scientists.
This is a fractal, a computer-generated mathematical
pattern that endlessly repeats itself at different scales.

A NEW WORLD

The Science of Today

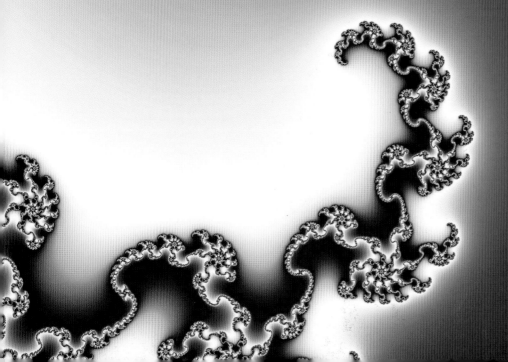

TOWARDS THE END

OF THE 20TH

CENTURY,

SCIENTISTS

BEGAN TO

DISCOVER

THAT THE UNIVERSE

IS STRANGER

THAN ANYONE IN

EARLIER CENTURIES

COULD HAVE

IMAGINED.

OUR SCIENTIFIC WORLD

OVER THE LAST FEW DECADES, SCIENCE HAS BECOME EVER MORE IMPORTANT TO US ALL. IN FACT, MOST OF US RELY ON SCIENTIFIC ADVANCES FOR THE SMOOTH RUNNING OF OUR EVERYDAY LIVES.

Scientists have unlocked the secrets of life, found out how to make materials that have whatever properties we might want them to have, and learned how to travel into space. Scientific discoveries have made our lives more comfortable, but they can be dangerous too, leading to new weapons and deadly accidents. So it is natural that some people fear or mistrust science. However, without science and scientists, we would still be living in caves.

▲ *After thousands of years of only being able to see objects in outer space through telescopes, people can now travel into space, and robots can reach distant planets and send back information.*

LOOK CLOSER

Although more people work in science than ever before, there are fewer individual famous scientists. This is because today's breakthroughs are usually made by teams of scientists.

TELEPORTATION

Working on the theories of Einstein, Bohr and Heisenberg, today's scientists discovered that the Universe is 'entangled'. This means that every part of the Universe is connected in a mysterious way to every other part. Technology based on this idea has allowed scientists to move the properties of one atom to another, which in turn will allow superfast computers to be built. Eventually, this might lead to people 'teleporting' – disappearing from one place and appearing in another.

▲ A mathematical theory that could predict the weather was developed at the beginning of the 20th century by Vilhelm Bjerknes. His theory could not be used for weather forecasting until advanced computers were developed in the late 20th century.

There are more than 6.5 billion people in the world, and the number is increasing.

Without scientific farming methods, the Earth could not support so many people.

LINUS PAULING

Linus Pauling really made his mark on the world. He is the only person ever to have been awarded two unshared Nobel prizes – for Chemistry and for Peace.

As a student, Pauling paid his way through college in America by teaching the courses he had been taught the previous year. He gave lectures and researched for 70 years, developing many different theories. In 1954, he received the Nobel Prize for Chemistry for his work using special X-ray techniques to discover more about the structure of chemicals and how they bond. Pauling also investigated the structure of proteins, revealing that the disease sickle cell anaemia is caused by a genetic defect. In 1962, he was awarded the Nobel Peace Prize for his years of campaigning against nuclear warfare and 'against all warfare as a means of solving international conflicts'.

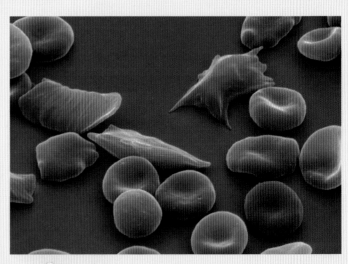

▲ Pauling studied sickle cell anaemia by examining the crescent-shaped blood cells affected by the disease.

◀ Pauling was not always right in his calculations. This is a model of his incorrect DNA triple helix, proposed in 1952.

Pauling was often criticized because of the great intuitive leaps in many of his theories.

He was an exciting lecturer, and would often drift into completely unrelated subjects.

PAULING THE CHILD

He loved reading when he was young – so much so that his father actually wrote a letter to a local paper inviting suggestions of additional books for him to read. Linus' friend, Lloyd Jeffress, had a small chemical laboratory in his bedroom and his experiments were an inspiration for Linus. When Linus went to high school, he continued to experiment, borrowing equipment from wherever he could find it. However, he did not get a high school diploma because he missed some classes. The school finally awarded Linus the diploma 45 years later, after he had been given two Nobel Prizes!

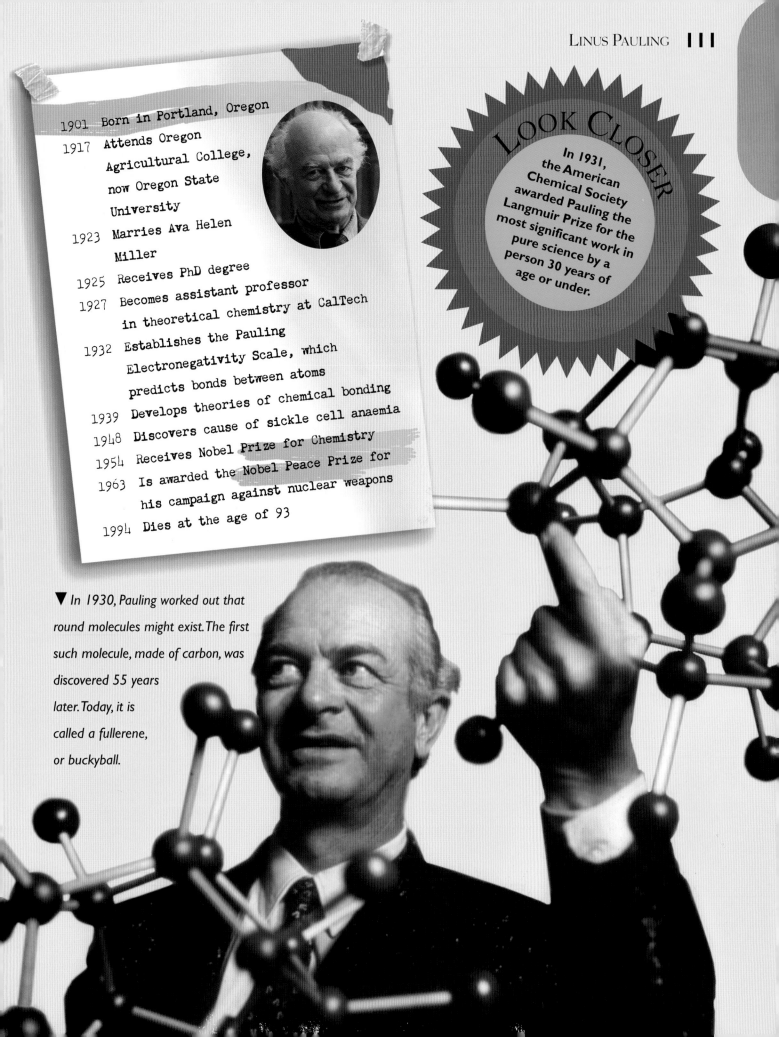

1901 Born in Portland, Oregon
1917 Attends Oregon
      Agricultural College,
      now Oregon State
      University
1923 Marries Ava Helen
      Miller
1925 Receives PhD degree
1927 Becomes assistant professor
      in theoretical chemistry at CalTech
1932 Establishes the Pauling
      Electronegativity Scale, which
      predicts bonds between atoms
1939 Develops theories of chemical bonding
1948 Discovers cause of sickle cell anaemia
1954 Receives Nobel Prize for Chemistry
1963 Is awarded the Nobel Peace Prize for
      his campaign against nuclear weapons
1994 Dies at the age of 93

LOOK CLOSER

In 1931, the American Chemical Society awarded Pauling the Langmuir Prize for the most significant work in pure science by a person 30 years of age or under.

▼ In 1930, Pauling worked out that round molecules might exist. The first such molecule, made of carbon, was discovered 55 years later. Today, it is called a fullerene, or buckyball.

Barbara McClintock

BARBARA MCCLINTOCK'S MOTHER THOUGHT HER INTEREST IN SCIENCE WAS NOT 'APPROPRIATE FEMININE BEHAVIOUR'. AND THAT WAS JUST THE START OF HER PROBLEMS! ALTHOUGH SHE WAS SCIENTIFICALLY SUCCESSFUL AT CORNELL UNIVERSITY, THE ONLY SUBJECT THERE IN WHICH WOMEN COULD BE PROFESSORS WAS HOME ECONOMICS.

McClintock moved to Missouri University but had to move again when it became clear that she would not be made a professor there either.

She struggled for scientific recognition partly because she worked in such a new area. Her interest was in genes, and her key discovery was 'jumping genes' that could move around from place to place, changing the other genes with which they came into contact. Eventually, other scientists discovered that she was correct and she was awarded a Nobel Prize.

1902 Born in Hartford, USA

1919 Studies botany at Cornell University

1931 Publishes first genetic map for maize

1944 Becomes only the third woman elected to the US National Academy of Sciences

1940s Discovers jumping genes

1960s Her work becomes well-known

1971 Is awarded the US National Medal of Science

1983 Is awarded the Nobel Prize for Medicine

1992 Dies in Huntington, USA

LOOK CLOSER

McClintock used jumping genes to control the way living things look. Today, scientists control genes so well that they could produce creatures that would look completely alien to us.

▲ *A mutant is a creature with altered genes. These make it different to others of the same species. Some mutant lobsters have mutant genes that make them blue.*

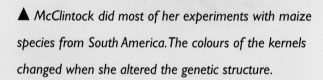

▲ *McClintock did most of her experiments with maize species from South America. The colours of the kernels changed when she altered the genetic structure.*

Jumping genes can result in the production of new, mutated creatures.

Mutants are sometimes better adapted and can survive better than other creatures.

The mutants replace the others. This is part of the process of evolution.

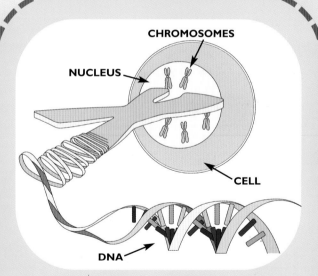

GENES AND CHROMOSOMES

Each of us is made of trillions of cells, and most of these have a central area called a nucleus. The nucleus contains structures called chromosomes, which in turn contain parts called genes. Each chromosome is made of a molecule called DNA (see page 116).

JONAS SALK

AT A TIME WHEN MANY PEOPLE, BOTH YOUNG AND OLD, WERE DYING FROM OR BEING CRIPPLED BY POLIO, AN AMERICAN DOCTOR CALLED JONAS SALK DEVELOPED A LIFE-SAVING VACCINATION.

In 1947, Jonas was working at the University of Pittsburgh as the head of the Virus Research Laboratory. He was conducting research into a vaccine for influenza, but at the same time began work on fighting polio. He knew that the polio virus attacked the nervous system and could cause breathing muscles to become paralyzed. He found a way to trigger an immune response, allowing sufferers to fight the virus. In 1954, national testing began on two million children, aged six to nine, known as the Polio Pioneers.

LOOK CLOSER

Salk could have made a great deal of money by patenting his vaccine. However, he believed that it belonged to the public, who had donated millions of dollars to his research.

▼ Some polio victims, including this two-year-old girl and man aged 45, had to use a machine called an 'iron lung' to breathe for them.

1914 Born in New York

1938 Begins work on an influenza vaccine

1939 Graduates from the School of Medicine, New York University

1942 Works as a staff physician at the Mount Sinai School of Medicine, New York

1947 Moves to University of Pittsburgh to head Virus Research Laboratory

1950s Designs and tests polio vaccine

1955 Begins immunization programme

1965 Establishes the Salk Institute for Biological Studies, La Jolla, California

1995 Dies at the age of 80

In 1952, at the height of the polio epidemics in the USA, there were 57,628 cases of the disease.

In the two years following the vaccine becoming available, the number of cases dropped by 85-90%.

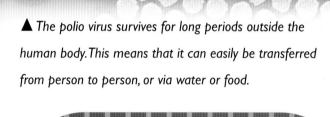

▲ The polio virus survives for long periods outside the human body. This means that it can easily be transferred from person to person, or via water or food.

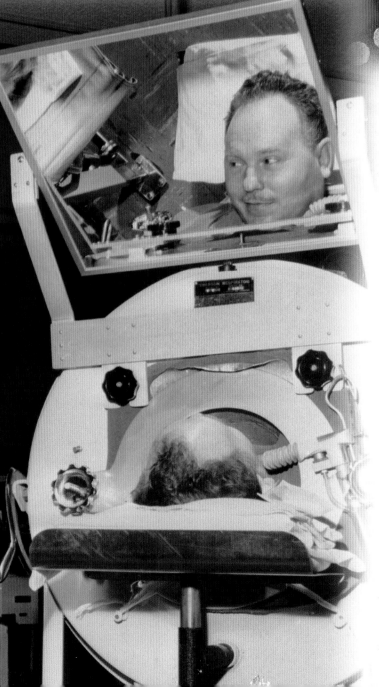

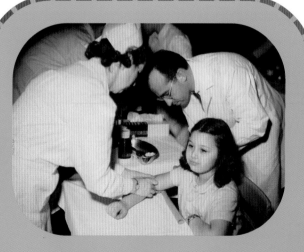

VACCINATION

In 1955, Salk began the polio immunization programme in elementary schools in Pittsburgh. Every child aged between six and nine was immunized. Here, Salk and a nurse are giving the vaccine to one of the Polio Pioneers, a girl at Sunnyside School.

WATSON, CRICK AND FRANKLIN

TOGETHER, SCIENTISTS JAMES WATSON (AMERICAN, 1928–), FRANCIS CRICK (BRITISH, 1916–2004) AND ROSALIND FRANKLIN (BRITISH, 1920–58) DISCOVERED THE SECRETS OF THE MOLECULES OF LIFE. YET FRANKLIN NEVER WORKED WITH CRICK AND WATSON ON DNA.

Franklin had built a special instrument to help study the structure of DNA, the molecule which controls every living thing on the planet. When Watson and Crick found out about her work, they used it to complete their model of DNA. Franklin's work certainly influenced their findings and they used her data, but she never worked directly with either Watson or Crick. The DNA structure the two scientists decided on was exactly right, and one of the greatest of all scientific breakthroughs.

In 1962, Watson, Crick and Maurice Wilkins shared a Nobel Prize for their discovery.

Wilkins had worked on the structure of DNA at the same time as Franklin.

The Prize can only be given to living scientists, and Franklin had died in 1958.

▲ DNA (deoxyribonucleic acid) is an enormous molecule, containing millions of atoms, joined together in a complicated repeating pattern. Unravelling its structure was a huge achievement.

▲ After her work on DNA, Franklin studied the tobacco mosaic virus, which sometimes behaves like a crystal and sometimes like a living thing.

THE HUMAN GENOME

DNA molecules join together to form chromosomes, and humans have 23 of these, each containing trillions of atoms. Nearly 40 years after helping to disentangle the structure of the DNA molecule, an enormous worldwide 'Human Genome' project began the task of mapping every detail of human chromosomes. James Watson was the project's first leader.

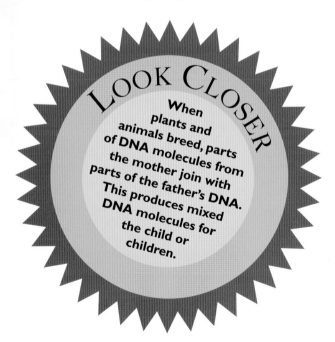

LOOK CLOSER

When plants and animals breed, parts of DNA molecules from the mother join with parts of the father's DNA. This produces mixed DNA molecules for the child or children.

▶ Watson and Crick are pictured with their model of DNA. Working with Maurice Wilkins, they raced against Linus Pauling (see page 110) to be the first to work out the structure.

STEPHEN HAWKING

STEPHEN HAWKING IS A LEADING EXPERT ON BLACK HOLES, AND HAS DEVELOPED MANY NEW THEORIES ABOUT THEM. HE HAS ALSO HELPED TO BUILD THEORIES ABOUT GRAVITY AS WELL AS ABOUT THE WHOLE UNIVERSE.

When Hawking was 21, he was diagnosed with motor neurone disease and given two years to live. He has defied all expectations and, in 2009, celebrated his 67th birthday. The disease means that Hawking has to use a motorized wheelchair, and he speaks using a computerized artificial voice.

Hawking has suggested a whole new way of understanding the beginning and end of time as parts of the Universe, a bit like the South Pole, which is the end of the Earth but also part of it.

1942 Born in Oxford, England

1963 Is diagnosed with motor neurone disease

1970 Predicts the existence of Hawking Radiation

1974 Is elected as a Fellow of the Royal Society in the UK

1979 Becomes Lucasian Professor at Cambridge University

1985 Begins to rely entirely on computer speech

1988 Publishes *A Brief History of Time*

2005 Publishes a revised book, *A Briefer History of Time*

◀ *Hawking is the Lucasian Professor of Mathematics at Cambridge University. He is in distinguished company – Isaac Newton and Charles Babbage have also held the post.*

Hawking wrote one of the most popular science books that has ever been published.

Called *A Brief History of Time*, it was a best-seller for 237 weeks.

LOOK CLOSER

Hawking has appeared on many television shows, including Red Dwarf, Star Trek: The Next Generation, The Simpsons and Futurama. He has also appeared in the film Superhero Movie.

▲ A view, taken by the Hubble Telescope, of the early Universe, not very long after the beginning of time. Hawking has developed theories about how time began.

BLACK HOLES

Astronomers used to think that nothing at all can escape a black hole. However, through his work Hawking has discovered that black holes (left) produce what is now called 'Hawking Radiation'. This means that small black holes gradually heat up and eventually disappear in a burst of heat and light. Large black holes, on the other hand, get colder as time passes. Hawking also suggested that the cores of black holes might possibly be 'bridges' to tiny 'baby universes'.

TIM BERNERS-LEE

MILLIONS OF PEOPLE USE THE WORLD WIDE WEB MANY TIMES A DAY, FOR EVERYTHING FROM INFORMATION AND RESEARCH TO SHOPPING. ITS INVENTOR IS THE ENGLISH COMPUTER SCIENTIST TIMOTHY BERNERS-LEE.

Before the Web was invented, computers all over the world were linked together in various ways (this network of computers is now called the Internet) but there was no simple way for them to send and receive information to each other. Berners-Lee studied ways to do this, and in 1980 built ENQUIRE. This was an experimental version of the World Wide Web that used a new approach to linking documents together. In 1989 CERN, one of the world's biggest laboratories, also had the largest number of Internet connections in Europe. Berners-Lee decided to try his new approach there. It was highly successful and the world was never the same again.

In 1993 there were only 623 websites in existence around the world.

Just three years later, the number of websites had mushroomed to about 100,000.

Today, there are well over 100 million, and more are being created every day.

AN INTERNET FIRST

This is the equipment that Berners-Lee used to launch the World Wide Web. It is now preserved in Microcosm, the science museum in CERN, Switzerland. Berners-Lee chose not to become a billionaire when he decided not to patent the Web.

◀ *Second Life is a 'virtual' world on the World Wide Web. People who use it create online versions of themselves called 'avatars'. Avatars can do practically anything, from partying to flying.*

LOOK CLOSER

Berners-Lee named his new system ENQUIRE after a book called Enquire Within Upon Everything, because the idea of both was that they should contain all useful knowledge.

▼ *In the beginning, few people had access to the World Wide Web. Today, businesses and families make use of it all the time to find out information, write emails, video conference or simply chat to friends.*

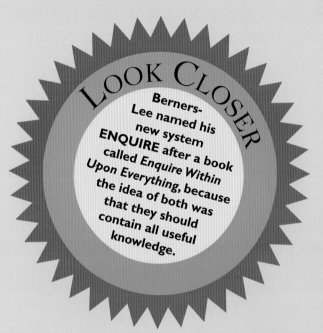

1955   Born in London, England

1980   Builds ENQUIRE system

1989   Proposes World Wide Web

1991   Launches first website, built at CERN, Switzerland

1994   Founds the World Wide Web Consortium, which helps the Web to develop, at Massachusetts Institute of Technology, USA

2004   Is first recipient of Finland's Millennium Technology Prize

2009   Elected member of the National Academy of Sciences

MORE SCIENTISTS

Over the last 2,500 years, there have been countless scientists who have made amazing discoveries. In this book, it has only been possible to look at a few of these scientists in detail, either because of the special importance of their work or the interesting lives that they led. However, some other major scientists are described briefly below.

THALES (C.625–C.550 BCE)

was a Greek philosopher and politician. He is the first person known to have developed a theory of the Universe, which he believed was based on water. Thales is also said to have predicted a solar eclipse, and fallen down a well because he was looking at the stars.

DEMOCRITUS (C.470–C.400 BCE)

believed that everything is made of atoms. Of the many scientific books this Greek philosopher wrote, only fragments remain. He was known as 'the laughing philosopher' because he was apparently amused by the weird things people do.

HIPPOCRATES (C.460–C.370 BCE)

was a Greek physician who became known as the 'father of medicine'. His efforts to base medicine on science rather than on magic marked an important turning-point in science, even though the treatments he suggested are mostly wrong. Many doctors today still take the Hippocratic Oath, swearing to work for the good of their patients.

EUCLID (C.330–C.260 BCE)

was a Greek mathematician who wrote a series of 13 books on geometry called *The Elements*, some parts of which were still used in schools in the early 20th century. Almost nothing is known about his life, except that, when asked by Ptolemy I of Egypt whether it was really necessary to read *The Elements* to learn geometry, Euclid is supposed to have said, 'There is no royal road to knowledge.'

EMPEDOCLES (C.270–C.190 BCE)

developed the earliest known theory of the elements, though it included only four – earth, air, fire and water – none of which are actually elements. Though incorrect, versions of this Greek philosopher's theory survived for over 2,000 years. Empedocles was also a biologist, and believed that living things evolved. It is said that he died by jumping into a volcano to prove that he would be taken to heaven by the gods.

GALEN (129–199 CE)

was a Greek-born physician to four Roman emperors, and travelled throughout the Roman Empire to carry out research into medicine and biology. He managed to make many discoveries about the human body, even though human dissection was forbidden. Though a lot of his treatments were actually ineffective, they were accepted and used by doctors for more than 1,500 years.

HYPATIA (C.370–415)

of Alexandria was a Greek scholar and one of the first known female scientists. She was a mathematician as well as an astronomer, but none of her writings survive. She was murdered by a mob.

ALHAZEN (965–1040)

was an expert in physics, mathematics, astronomy and medicine. He was born in Basra (now in Iraq). His experiments with light showed how vision works and why the sky stays light after sunset. In about 1015, Caliph Al-Hakim asked him to control the waters of the River Nile. When he failed, Alhazen pretended to be mad to avoid punishment.

ANDREAS VESALIUS (1514–1564)

was a teacher of human anatomy who dissected human bodies to show his students how they worked. He became physician to King Charles I of Spain, but his new ideas were unpopular.

ROBERT HOOKE (1635–1703)

helped to found the Royal Society in London. He set up experiments, built equipment and argued with Isaac Newton. Hooke invented an air-pump and improved versions of both the telescope and microscope.

ALEXANDER VON HUMBOLDT (1769-1859)

was a German naturalist who combined science and travel by making a scientific expedition to Central and South America that lasted five years and covered 10,000 km. Humboldt studied the Earth's magnetism, ocean currents and weather, and developed the weather mapping system that we use today. He also set a world record by climbing the 6,876 m-high Chimborazo volcano in Ecuador.

KARL FRIEDRICH GAUSS (1777-1855)

was a very talented mathematician. He was born to a poor German family and corrected his father's errors in arithmetic when he was only three years old. The Duke of Brunswick heard of his skills and paid for his education. Gauss made major mathematical discoveries from the age of 15, and was a physicist and astronomer as well. He was able to track down an asteroid (a small body that orbits the Sun) that had been discovered the previous year but then lost when it passed behind the Sun.

MAX PLANCK (1858-1947)

was a German physicist whose work marked the beginning of a new sort of physics, quantum theory. Planck discovered that the way that glowing objects behave can only be explained through the idea that energy can exist in the form of tiny units, now called quanta. 'Planck's constant', one of the most important numbers in science, shows how the frequency of radiation (which might be light or other things such as radio waves or X-rays) relates to the energy of a quantum of that radiation. But Planck found it very difficult to believe his own discovery, and

it was left to Einstein, Bohr, Heisenberg, Schrödinger and many other scientists to build the new physics that he had begun. Strongly opposed to the Nazis, Planck actually met with Adolf Hitler in 1933 and tried to argue against his policies.

ALFRED WEGENER (1880-1930)

was a German geologist who was mainly interested in meteorology, the science of weather. However, his most important discovery was continental drift – the idea that, millions of years ago, all the present continents were joined together as a single supercontinent, called Pangaea. Few scientists agreed with him. But by the 1960s, an explanation, and more evidence, had been found and continental drift is now an accepted fact. Wegener's researches took him on several expeditions to Greenland, and on one of these, he died out on the ice.

ERWIN SCHRÖDINGER (1887-1961)

was an Austrian physicist. He developed an equation to describe the movement of tiny particles. He used it to correctly predict the energy levels in a hydrogen atom. Schrödinger always liked to travel with hiking boots and rucksack – and was almost refused entry to an important scientific conference as a result! In 1933, he received the Nobel Prize for Physics.

WOLFGANG PAULI (1900-1958)

discovered many of the laws that govern the behaviour of electrons, the particles that occupy nearly all the space in atoms. This Austrian physicist also predicted the existence of a particle called a neutrino. Though a brilliant theoretical scientist, Pauli was also famous for the 'Pauli effect' – accidental damage to scientific apparatus that seemed to happen when he was nearby!

ENRICO FERMI (1901-1954)

was an Italian physicist who helped to develop theories that explain the behaviour of atoms and the particles from which they are made. Fermi was in charge of the United States secret wartime Manhattan Project, which built the world's first nuclear reactor in a Chicago squash court. He became known as the 'father of the atomic bomb'.

HIDEKI YUKAWA (1907-1981)

was a Japanese physicist who explained how the nuclei of atoms are held together. Yukawa also predicted the existence of a new kind of particle, called a pi-meson, and was awarded a Nobel Prize when it was discovered. After World War II, Yukawa joined with other scientists to try to rid the world of nuclear weapons.

SUBRAMANYAN CHANDRASEKHAR (1910-1995)

was born in India and later became an American citizen. Chandrasekhar explained why massive stars turn into white dwarfs, neutron stars or black holes when they run out of fuel, and was awarded a Nobel Prize for his discoveries. Both an asteroid and an X-ray telescope have since been named after him.

ALAN TURING (1912-1954)

was a British mathematician who is often described as the father of modern computer science. He imagined a 'Turing Machine', then went on to help build a real version of it – one of the world's first electronic computers. He used his mathematical skills to break German secret codes during World War II, but he was later persecuted for his homosexuality, which led to his suicide.

GLOSSARY

■ **ALCHEMY**
A mixture of science and magic, from which chemistry developed.

■ **ANATOMY**
The study of the structure of living things.

■ **ANTIBIOTICS**
Medicines that attack bacteria, which are tiny living things that cause some illnesses.

■ **ASTRONOMY**
The study of the stars, planets and other objects in space beyond Earth.

■ **ATOM**
A very tiny particle of matter. Atoms are part of the structure of every solid, liquid and gas.

■ **BIOLOGY**
The science of living things.

■ **BLACK HOLE**
The remains of a star. It has such a strong gravity that it sucks in every object around it. Not even light can escape.

■ **BOTANY**
The science of plants.

■ **CELL**
A microscopic structure that forms the basic unit of matter in all living things.

■ **CHEMISTRY**
The science of materials.

■ **CHROMOSOME**
Structures inside cells that control the way that living things work.

■ **CLASSIFICATION**
The organization of living things into a system of categories according to their origin, structure etc.

■ **COMBUSTION**
The process of burning.

■ **DNA**
Deoxyribonucleic acid – the chemical from which chromosomes are made.

■ **ECLIPSE**
The blocking of the light from the Sun or Moon. A solar eclipse is when the Moon moves between the Sun and Earth. A lunar eclipse is when the Earth moves between the Sun and the Moon.

■ **ELECTROMAGNETIC SPECTRUM**
The range of different types of radiation, including gamma rays, x-rays, ultraviolet radiation, light, infrared radiation, microwaves and radio waves.

■ **ELECTRON**
A tiny particle that carries an electrical charge. Atoms contain electrons.

■ **ELEMENT**
A material that is made up of atoms that are of the same kind. Elements cannot be reduced to simpler substances.

■ **EVOLUTION**
The gradual change in animals and plants over generations.

■ **EXTINCTION**
The dying out of a species.

■ **GENE**
A section of a chromosome that controls one or more features of a living thing.

■ **GEOLOGY**
The science of the rocks and other materials that make up the Earth.

■ **GRAVITY**
The pull of every object on every other object. It is usually only noticeable when one of the objects is very large.

■ **INFRARED RADIATION**
Part of the electromagnetic spectrum. Some infrared radiation can be felt as heat.

■ **INTERNET**
A vast computer network that links computers all over the world.

■ **LENS**
An object that changes the shape of a beam of light that passes through it.

■ **LIGHT WAVE**
The pattern of changing electric and magnetic fields that we see as light.

■ **MAGNETISM**
The force that pulls some objects together or pushes them apart.

■ **MATHEMATICS**
The science of numbers, shapes and amounts, and of their relationships.

■ **MICROSCOPE**
An instrument used to make a small object look larger.

■ **MOLECULE**
A tiny structure, made of at least two atoms. Molecules are the smallest units of most materials.

■ **MUTANT**
A living thing that is different to other members of its species because of genetic changes.

■ **NATURALIST**
Someone who studies living things.

■ **NUCLEAR POWER**
Power released by changes in the nuclei of atoms.

■ **NUCLEUS**

The core of an atom, or a structure that is found in most cells and that controls them.

■ **PARTICLE**

A tiny object, too small to be seen. Atoms are particles and so are the objects atoms are made of, such as electrons.

■ **PASTEURIZATION**

The process by which food or drinks are made safe by heating them to kill bacteria.

■ **PHILOSOPHY**

The study of general ideas (such as truth, beauty or time) by means of reasoned argument.

■ **PHYSICS**

The science of energy and matter.

■ **PRISM**

An optical prism bends light and can split white light into a spectrum.

■ **QUANTUM (PLURAL QUANTA)**

A tiny packet of energy. Quanta of light are called photons.

■ **QUANTUM MECHANICS**

The area of physics that explains how matter and

energy behave when the distances, times or amounts involved are very small.

■ **RADIOACTIVITY**

Dangerous particles and rays given out by some materials.

■ **SPECIES**

A group of animals or plants that look alike and can breed with one another.

■ **SPECTRUM**

Pattern of colours into which white light is split, for example by a prism.

■ **TECHNOLOGY**

The practical use of science.

■ **TELESCOPE**

Instrument that makes distant objects appear larger and brighter.

■ **THERMOMETER**

Instrument that measures how hot or cold something is.

■ **WEBSITE**

Collection of documents (called webpages) that forms part of the World Wide Web.

■ **X–RAY**

Part of the electromagnetic spectrum. X-rays pass through flesh and other materials, so they are used to look inside living things and other objects.

FURTHER READING

THE ILLUSTRATED TIMELINE OF SCIENCE
by Sidney Strickland and Eliza Strickland (Sterling Publishing Company Inc., 2007)

THE SCIENCE BOOK
by Peter Tallack (Cassell and Company, 2003)

EYEWITNESS: GREAT SCIENTISTS
by Jacqueline Fortey (Dorling Kindersley, 2007)

DARWIN & OTHER SERIOUSLY SUPER SCIENTISTS
by Mike Goldsmith (Scholastic, 2009)

SUFFERING SCIENTISTS
by Nick Arnold (Scholastic, 2000)

WEBSITES

For biographies of scientists, go to:
http://scienceworld.wolfram.com/biography/
AND
www.blupete.com/Literature/Biographies/Science/Scients.htm

Take a look at the Science Museum, London's online science material:
http://www.sciencemuseum.org.uk/onlinestuff.aspx

Visit BBC science online:
http://www.bbc.co.uk/schools/websites/4_11/site/science.shtml

Try out some science experiments and projects:
http://www.kids-science-experiments.com/

For people and events in science history, try:
http://www.todayinsci.com/

INDEX

ACKNOWLEDGEMENTS

AKG Images: Erich Lessing 60bl; **Alamy:** Robert Bird 51t, Lordprice Collection 42-43, Medical On Line 99tl, Natural History Museum 53t, North Wind Picture Archive 15bl, Photo Researchers 100tr, The Print Collection 49t, Glyn Thomas 57b; **Art Archive:** Musee Archaeologique Naples/Alfredo Dagli Orti 16tr, Musee National des Techniques, Paris/Gianni Dagli Orti 61t, Univeristy Library Istanbul/Gianni Dalgi Orti 22-23; **Bridgeman Art Library:** Private Collection 30, 36, Private Collection/Archives Charmet 27br, Science Museum, London, UK 47b; **CERN:** 94-95; **Corbis:** 68b, Gary Bell, 9t, Bettmann 8t, 22bl, 31br, 37tl, 38-39, 44, 62-63, 68-69, 79tl, 86tr, 89bl, 89-99, 114-115, 115br, Stefano Bianchetti 29, Blue Lantern Studio 4b, 14, Christel Gerstenberg 19tl, Diego Goldberg/Sygma 112t, Historical Picture Archives 26, Hulton Deutsch Collection 88-89, 105bl, Tim Klein/Stock This Way 7b, Frans Lanting 72b, Georgina Lowell 90-91, Jaques Morell /Kipa 78-79, Jose Luis Palaez 121bl, Douglas Peebles 9b, Andy Rain/EPA 74-75, Roger Ressmeyer 21tr, Stapleton Collection 39t, Eberhard Streuchen 6-7, The Art Archive 27tl, 37tr, The Gallery Collection 13, 34l, 40-41, 45t, Visuals Unlimited 115tr, Ron Watts 10-11; **Getty Images:** Bridgeman Art Library: 66, Hulton Archive 40c, 92, National Geographic 34-35, 103b, Tim Graham Photo Library 15tl; **JI Unlimited:** 5t, 17, 16bl, 28cl, 31bl, **Kobal Collection:** Amblin/Universal 75cl; **Mary Evans Picture Library:** 57tl, 67bl, 70-71, 70bl; **NASA:** 39cr, 47t, 85t,

GSFC/GOES 109, Les Bossinas 93, Lunar Orbiter IV 55tl, Robert Williams & Hubble Field Team 119t; **Photolibrary.com:** SGM 101; **Photoshot:** World Illustrated 56; **Rex Features:** Sipa Press 120/121; **Science Photo Library:** 33b, 46c, 46br, 50, 59br, 61cr, 67t, 73bl, 76, 77tl, 80cl, 80cr, 83tr, 83cl, 84br, American Institute of Physics 51br, 104bl, Andrew Lambert Photography 105br, A. Barrington Brown 117br, Bluestone 77cr, Dr Jeremy Burgess 48t, CCI Archives 51bl, Cern 120c, Jean-Loup Charmet 32b, 52tr, 62bl, 63br, Lynette Cook 108, Colin Cuthbert 82, Victor De Schwanberg 97b, Emilio Segre Visual Archive/American Institute of Physics 102-103, Eye of Science 110ct, Mark Garlick 59tr, Tony & Daphne Hallas 102bl, Thomas Hollymoon 111b, James King-Holmes 77bl, 117tr, Leonard Lessin 79cr, Peter Manzel 113, Hank Morgan 121br, NASA/ESA/STSCI/R. Kennicut, U. Arizona 103tr, National Library of Medicine 87tr, Omikron 111t, David Parker 53b, 59tl, Pekka Parviainen 33t, Pasieka 5b, 116, Royal Astronomical Society 58bl, Royal Observatory, Edinburgh 32tr; Science Source 96, 117tl, Dr Seth Shostak 119b, Takeshi Takahara 104/105, Sheila Terry 12, 45cr, 58-59, University of Pittsburgh 114cl, Detlev Van Ravenswaay 24-25; **Shutterstock:** 15cr, Linda Armstrong 54-55t, Laurent Dambies 28br, C. Florin 104-107, Stephen Girimont 37b, Roman Krochuk 31t, Andreas Mayer 6b, Anna Subbotina 54b, Denis Vrublevski 52tl; **Science & Society Picture Library:** NMeM 81, Science Museum 20tr, 110cb;

Topham: 94-95, 72tr, 73tr, 89br, 98bl, Ann Ronan Picture Library/HIP 63t, Charles Walker 38c, E&E Images/HIP 71br, David R. Frazier/The Image Works 8b, David Gamble 118bl, John Hedgecoe 118tr, Roger-Viollet 19tr, 99b, The Granger Collection 18-19, 71tr, 85b, 97tl, Ullstein Bild 84bl, 94bl, 94br, 95b; **University of Pensylvannia Libraries:** Edgar Fahs Smith Collection 48b, 60cr, 69br; **Uppsala Univeristy Astronomical Observatory:** 54t; **Wellcome Library, London:** 23br; **Wikimedia:** 20br, 21bl, 35t, 100bl, Uppsala Celsius Observatory 55b, Steven G. Johnson 112b.

The Brown Reference Group has made every attempt to contact the copyright holders of all pictures used in this work. Please contact info@brownreference.com if you have any information identifying copyright ownership.

MANAGING EDITOR: MIRANDA SMITH
EDITORIAL DIRECTOR: LINDSEY LOWE
CHILDREN'S PUBLISHER: ANNE O'DALY
DESIGNER: ARVIND SHAH
DESIGN MANAGER: DAVID POOLE
CREATIVE DIRECTOR: JENI CHILD
PICTURE RESEARCHERS: CLARE NEWMAN, SEAN HANNAWAY
PICTURE MANAGER: SOPHIE MORTIMER